# BEHIND CLOSED DOORS

# BEHIND CLOSED DOORS

## Teachers and the Role of the Teachers' Lounge

Miriam Ben-Peretz
and
Shifra Schonmann

Foreword by Philip W. Jackson

State University of New York Press

Published by
State University of New York Press, Albany



Printed in the United States of America



For information, address State University of New York Press, State University Plaza, Albany, N.Y., 12246

Production by Diane Ganeles
Marketing by Patrick Durocher

Library of Congress Cataloging-in-Publication Data

Ben-Peretz, Miriam.
Behind closed doors : teachers and the role of the teachers' lounge / Miriam Ben-Peretz and Shifra Schonmann.
p. cm.
Includes bibliographical references.
ISBN 0-7914-4447-3 (alk. paper). — ISBN 0-7914-4448-1 (pbk. : alk. paper)
1. Teachers—Professional relationships. 2. Teachers—Social conditions. 3. Teachers' lounges. 4. Teachers—In-service training. I. Schonmann, Shifra. II. Title.
LB1775.B45 2000
371.14'8—dc21 99-15031
CIP

10 9 8 7 6 5 4 3 2 1

# Contents

# Foreword

What happens when groups of Israeli classroom teachers get together for extended time in the staff rooms and lounges of their own school? What do they talk about? How do they relate to one another? What value do they attach to their experiences while there? What light, if any, do their exchanges shed on the nature of teaching?

Such are the questions that Miriam Ben-Peretz and Shifra Schonmann energetically address in this thought-provoking book. To do so they employ a variety of data-gathering techniques, including direct observation, video-taping, interviews, personal essays, and questionnaires. They also borrow liberally from other investigators, making especially good use of terms and concepts developed by the cultural anthropologists: Erving Goffman, E. T. Hall, and Victor Turner. They further do not hesitate to use figurative language, particularly that of metaphor, to probe the deeper meaning of their observations.

What do all of these probes reveal about the goings on in teachers' lounges? To answer that question in depth one must read on, for only a complete perusal of the pages to follow will yield an adequate account. Yet there remains a briefer and quicker answer, which I feel free to give at this point without risking disclosure of any of the secrets contained in the material to follow.

Having just finished reading *Behind Closed Doors,* my answer to what goes on in teachers' lounges reduces to this: "Lots of things—far more than most outsiders would guess."

With doors closed to most intruders, especially to students, teachers behave in ways that contrast markedly with their classroom demeanor. They talk shop constantly. They exchange ideas. They argue about methods. They complain about school administrators. They express frustration and anger over classroom conditions. They break into tears. They rage and pound tables. They soothe one another. They also squabble and divide into cliques. They make back-biting remarks about each other. They gossip and joke and sometimes jointly celebrate a joyous event. Above all, they relax. They let their hair down, as the expression goes, and they sometimes fuss with putting it back up. They drink a lot of coffee.

The trouble with such a brief catalogue of activity is that it says nothing about what Dewey would call "conditions and consequences." It does not begin to identify the conditions that give rise to desirable or undesirable patterns of interaction in the lounges. Nor does it say anything about the long-term consequences of the teachers' having been there.

To answer those more detailed and far more important questions, we must turn to the multifaceted data that Ben-Peretz and Schonmann present. With their help we must listen to what teachers say about their experiences in teachers' lounges. Through the researchers' eyes and those of their trained observers, we must watch how teachers behave when the lounge door is closed. To make sense of what our vicarious looking and listening tells us, we must also compare it with what we know about what happens within other informal and semi-private gathering places, such as the backstage of theaters, the locker rooms of athletic teams, the steamy kitchens of fancy restaurants. Ben-Peretz and Schonmann have much to say about some of those comparisons. They do not treat them all, needless to say but the comments they do offer certainly point their readers in the right direction.

What of the possibility of enabling all teachers, both novices and veterans, to make better use of the lounges their schools provide? Ben-Peretz and Schonmann address that question as well. They suggest ways of helping teachers in training to become better acquainted with the dynamics of what can and often does take place in such cloistered environments. Experienced teachers have no less to gain than do neophytes in giving thought to such matters, which is yet another reason for my calling their book thought-provoking.

Finally, what shall we foreign readers make of the fact that Ben-Peretz and Schonmann studied only Israeli teachers? Would their findings have come out exactly the same if they had gathered their data elsewhere? Almost certainly not. Cultural differences of unpredictable aspect would surely appear. Yet the detailed accounts contained in this book sound so familiar to me as an American that I have a hard time believing that much would change if the study were conducted in the schools of my own city. Moreover, I expect the same would be true of findings collected from other sites at home and abroad. Here, then, is a book that promises to enlighten us all. Read on.

Philip W. Jackson
Chicago

# Acknowledgments

This book is based on a study of teachers' lounges which lasted several years.

We are extremely grateful to the many teachers and principals who allowed us to get a glimpse behind the closed doors of their workplace and their lounges.

For their constructive comments on this work, we thank Prof. Moshe Silberstein, Tel Aviv University, and Dr. Yehudith Cais, University of Haifa. We are deeply grateful to Prof. Philip Jackson, University of Chicago, for his interest and for writing the foreword to this book.

Special thanks are due to Lois G. Patton, former Associate Director and Editor-in-Chief of SUNY Press, for her continuing support and encouragement. We wish to thank Priscilla Ross, Associate Director and Editor-in-Chief, for her advice and support, and Diane Ganeles, Senior Production Editor, for her careful and sensitive copyediting.

Thanks to Anat Zajdman for typing the first draft of our book and to Marion Lupu, for proofreading of the last draft.

Finally, we wish to express our deep and special gratitude to Menachem Shonmann and Moshe Ben-Peretz for their patient support throughout all stages of this work.

# Introduction

Teachers' lounges constitute an almost uncharted territory in the educational environment of schools. What happens in the lounge behind its closed doors? What kinds of interactions occur there? What functions does the lounge serve beyond being a place to relax between classes and, possibly, drink a cup of coffee? Is it a meaningless "non-place," lacking any real importance in the culture of schools? Or is it an integral part of school life, with far-reaching consequences for the well-being and success of teachers, administrators, and students? These are some of the questions addressed in this book.

Our own former practice as high school teachers provided us with ample experience of such lounges. Sometimes the lounge served as a refuge from the stress and problems of teaching. Personal friendships were formed and professional insights were shared there. At other times, the lounge became an arena for confrontations with colleagues or superiors. Overall it was an important element in our everyday working lives. As teacher educators and researchers, however, we focused mainly on the study of learners and learning, of teachers and teaching in the framework of the classroom, neglecting the teachers' lounge.

Only later in our attempts to understand the culture of schools did the lacuna concerning teachers' lounges cause a reawakening of our interest in an area which we regarded as a central component in the professional lives of teachers. The heart of school life lies in the teachers' lounge; therefore "deciphering" the events that take place there leads us to a better understanding of teaching as a profession. Our interest led us to a study of teachers' lounges.

Our investigation of the teachers' lounge is based on three assumptions:

1. The lounge is a defined and separate space in the school building; it is usually considered to be the teachers' own territory.
2. The teachers, as adults interacting in the lounge, create their own social organization.
3. The lounge is the natural site for the development of professional communities in schools.

Our first assumption concerns the nature of the lounge as a defined place in the school building, assigned for the use of teachers as adults (Hargreaves & Woods 1984). In Israel, the United States, Europe, South Africa, and many other countries, such a space is part of the regular school architecture. The special characteristics of such rooms might differ from country to country, and between different schools in the same country. These features are determined, to a certain extent, by the teachers using the lounge. This leads us to our second assumption that teachers, as adults, create their own social organization. The notion of a school culture and life in classrooms is treated extensively in educational literature, as in Jackson 1968; Lieberman & Miller 1984; and Rosenholtz 1989. In this book we see life in lounges as a subculture of adults, evolving through interactions based on collegiality, or its lack. Trust or mistrust, positive support or its denial, sharing in decision-making, humor or tragedy, and other elements of social organizations can also be seen there.

Our third assumption concerns the lounge as a natural site for the development of professional communities in school (McLaughlin 1994). The lounge (sometimes known as the staffroom or teachers' room) is usually the only place in the school devoted to the meeting of teachers at regular intervals, at specific times, sharing a common space. All these features serve to make the lounge a natural site for the development of professional communities.

On the basis of these assumptions we decided to start our inquiry by listening to teachers' perceptions of life in such rooms. Gaining insights into the centrality of lounges in teachers' lives we continued our study by viewing the lounge through conceptions of professional development, and the power of social relations among adults in school, using dramatic terms to deepen our understanding of these conceptions in the context of teachers' lounges. Some of these concepts are: catharsis; proxemics; the fourth wall; and conventions. The process of inquiry into the culture of lounges led us to the writing of this book.

One of the main aspects of school culture is the way in which teachers behave to each other professionally and socially, especially in the subculture of the lounge. During the course of the average day, the teachers spend almost all of their time with children, and it is extremely rare for a teacher to be physically alone. The amount of time teachers spend in face-to-face contact with each other is thus extremely small (Sarason 1996). By looking at the teachers' room as a place for face-to-face interaction between teachers, we direct attention to the potential of teachers to build communities. Cunningham & Gresco (1993) state that "culture-building requires that school leaders give attention to the informal subtle and symbolic aspects of school life, which shape the beliefs and actions of each employee within the system" (p. 35).

"The way we do things around here" is an important component of any school's culture. According to Sarason (1972), cultures differ from each other because of their distinct structures or patterns, which govern the rules and interrelationships within a specific setting. Sarason suggests that the "existing structure of a setting or culture defines the permissible ways in which goals and problems will be approached" (p. 12).

We focus on the social situations arising in the context of the social organizations in teachers' lounges, and on vignettes pertaining to the ways in which teachers approach problems and goals through interacting in their community.

Teachers in the lounge are regarded in our study as "learners," whether they are actually involved in formal professional development activities, or in informal exchanges with their colleagues. Teachers learn about students and modes of instruction, but also about the norms of collegiality that govern life in the lounge, and about supporting each other and coping with the manifold stresses of teaching. The lounge is the site for the development of "communal knowledge," which characterizes specific schools at specific times, thus creating a school ethos. As argued by Talbert & McLaughlin (1994): "Professionalism evolves within active learning communities of teachers" (p. 123). We felt that the ongoing activities in teachers' lounges with their "beehive" quality provide the appropriate environment for the creation of such communities, in which professional development accrues, and professional knowledge is created.

## The Development of Professional Knowledge

One may distinguish between professional knowledge inside and outside the classroom. Clandinin & Connelly (1995) view professional knowledge as comprising a landscape:

> Understanding professional knowledge as comprising a landscape calls for a notion of professional knowledge as composed of a wide variety of components and influenced by a wide variety of people, places and things. Because we see the professional knowledge landscape as composed of relationships among people, places, and things, we see it as both an intellectual and a moral landscape. (p. 4)

In their classrooms, teachers interact with students, are "*in charge*," are autonomous in their actions, expressing their personal practical knowledge that has arisen from experience and comprises a body of convictions and meanings, routines, and social acts, leading to certain kinds of instructional strategies and activities. Classrooms are in Schwab's (1970) terms practical places.

In communal places, such as teachers' lounges, teachers interact with their peers, with office holders such as principals, as well as with parents and other adults. Professional knowledge outside the classroom may be understood as a blend of practice and theory. Teachers bring to it their live stories of practice which, according to Clandinin & Connelly (1995) are "*secret stories*," which may be told to other teachers. Through telling and retelling their stories, teachers are able to reflect on their practice, and their professional knowledge develops and grows:

> Teachers need others in order to engage in conversations where stories can be told, reflected back, heard in different ways, retold, and relived in new ways in the safety and secrecy of the classroom. (p. 13)

Teachers lounges are sites where these conversations might be conducted. But lounges are also places which serve as a conduit for outside knowledge in the form of policy directives, information sessions, memos, and the like. Clandinin & Connelly (1995) view this part of the professional knowledge landscape as abstract in two senses. This knowledge is decontextualized, not based on people, events, or things. The existential world is not involved. Moreover, research conclusions and policy prescriptions reach teachers in the form of a "rhetoric of conclusions," codified outcomes of inquiry. Clandinin & Connelly argue that this knowledge acquires qualities of a "*sacred story.*" "Everything comes with a moral push with which teachers are expected to do something. This moral orientation and sense of persuasion are due to the sacred story which requires that the descriptive "is" of theoretical knowledge be transferred into a prescriptive "ought" in practice" (p. 11). According to Clandinin & Connelly, the boundary between classroom and the outer spaces is semipermeable. Teachers carry their narrative knowledge, their secret stories, with them outside their classrooms and the rhetoric of conclusions invades classroom life, creating dilemmas for teachers.

In this book we argue that the teachers' lounge constitutes a place in which they can find secure space and time for them to tell their secret stories with no need for "cover stories." At the same time "sacred stories" of external policies and school norms become part of the discourse, providing a space for consultation, debate, and even confrontation. Thus the boundaries between the personal professional knowledge, experiential and immediate, and the more abstract impersonal and distant professional knowledge which finds its way into the lounge are blurred and the dilemma described by Clandinin & Connelly might be resolved. The lounge is a haven for what Fullan & Hargreaves (1996) call interactive professionalism—which calls for opportunities to exercise judgment over issues of curriculum and teaching and to engage with the moral and social purposes of education. Collaborative cultures (Talbert & McLaughlin 1994) of teachers provide help and support in using shared expertise to solve the ongoing problems of professional practice.

When we speak of professional development, we speak about learning which, according to social learning theory, is based on social context, by observing and interacting with others (Schunk 1991). Individuals gain insights and understanding of their institutions through work-role performance and interaction with coworkers (Louis 1990).

As will be shown, this learning process takes place in teachers' lounges. Smylie (1995) states that one of the crucial conditions that may promote learning in the workplace concerns opportunities for individuals to work with and learn from others on an ongoing basis. It is our claim that teachers' lounges provide just such opportunities as teachers meet there regularly day after day. Fullan (1995) emphasizes this point by stating that

> continuous learning must be organically part and parcel of the culture of the school. (p. 258)

Our study was conducted in Israeli elementary, junior, and high schools. Teachers in Israel at all levels of schooling usually spend the breaks between classes in a common lounge, as there are no private spaces for them, nor is it customary for teachers to stay in their classrooms. Generally, the school day in Israel at all age levels starts around seven or eight A.M. and ends around one or two P.M. During this time there are three short breaks of ten minutes each, and one longer break of twenty to thirty minutes. Usually no lunch is served at school. Israeli teachers may have free periods during their teaching day and they tend to spend these periods in the lounge. These is no formal obligation for all teachers to start and complete their teaching at the same hours. One might, therefore, find teachers arriving early in the day or later. From this point of view the lounge serves as the entry and departure points in the teachers' day in school.

In spite of the localized context of our study we invite the reader to engage in the issues we raise and to examine the insights gained concerning teacher development and communities of adults in schools. Several concepts emerged in this study (such as the "norms of a 'good colleague'," "communal knowledge," "collective catharsis," "proxemics in the lounge") which reflect the value of the lounge as a space for the development of professional communities in schools, a space which provides a suitable context for the generation of valid knowledge about teaching. These concepts, along with other notions developed recently in pedagogical literature, such as the idea of communities of teachers as learners, provide a way of viewing the daily routines of teachers. Ways of viewing and ways of knowing teachers' lounges in Israel may serve as a basis for comparison with other cultures.

## The Inner Logic of the Book

In our first chapter we describe our various modes of inquiry, the data elicited through these diverse approaches, and the logic of the evolving issues and topics. The employment of a variety of inquiry models enabled us to tackle our subject from complementary perspectives.

Chapter 2: *Social Situations.* We analyze the social situation in the lounge, with its particular structures, such as norms of collegiality, and the concept of a "good colleague."

Doubting the "myth of the lonely teacher," we portray the interactive and closely knit nature of the social reality of teachers in the lounge.

Chapter 3: *Dramatic Language.* We apply dramatic terms to gain insights into the intricacies of teaching communities. Using this frame of reference, we combine the unique and the personal with the communal perspective, as exemplified by our concept of collective catharsis. Based on the stories of teachers, we discuss conventions and the nature and function of "collective catharsis" occurring in the lounge.

Chapter 4: *Blurring of Boundaries.* We analyze life in lounges as characterized by a blurring of boundaries between frontstage and backstage, between public and private time, providing the conceptual framework for understanding the dual function of lounges as a place of rest as well as a place of work. "Place" and "time" are two of the concepts treated in this chapter. Another term from the world of drama is "proxemics"; it explains the nature of interpersonal relationships in the confines of a small space. This leads us to discuss the physical reality in various lounges.

Chapter 5: *Metaphors and Monologues.* We move our lens to personal expressions of teachers writing about their lounges—in the form of metaphors and monologues. We focus on their voices, revealing the roles that these rooms play in their professional lives.

Chapter 6: *Teachers' Perceptions of Lounges and Student Achievement.* We relate teachers' responses to questionnaires about lounges with student achievement results, gaining insights into possible roles that the lounge can play in the overall culture of the school. Analysis of characteristics of lounges, as perceived by teachers, yielded three factors concerning possible functions of lounges: the social function; the political function; and the work function. Perceived spheres of the influence of lounges on different domains of life in schools are discussed. The relationship between teachers' perceptions of their lounges and student achievement is calculated and analyzed. This chapter was coauthored with Haggai Kupermintz. Turning our lenses in another direction, we observe the interactions between teachers and their superiors, the principals.

Chapter 7: *Principals in Teachers' Lounges: Intruders or Colleagues?* This chapter addresses the relationship between leadership modes of principals and the culture of teachers' lounges. Based on interviews with principals, potential conflict situations are presented. The reactions of teachers to the pressure of the presence of principals in the lounge are also discussed.

Chapter 8: *Professional Communities and Teachers' Development.* This chapter moves to a discussion of professional communities in schools and the development of teachers. In this chapter teachers are portrayed as learners in the lounge: they share, construct, and reconstruct a communal professional knowledge base which is school-specific. Thus, teachers' learning in lounges is not perceived as confined to instances of staff development through lectures or workshops, but grows through the interactions between teachers in their community of discourse.

Chapter 9: *Implications for Teacher Education.* The issues dealt with in the various chapters provide a holistic view of the role lounges play in schools. The inner logic of our book as described above leads us to a discussion of the implications of the study of the culture of lounges and teaching communities for teacher education programs. Two of the themes treated in this chapter are societal forces and gender issues. Some suggestions are made for including the topic of teachers' lounges in the curriculum of teacher education programs.

Epilogue: *Paradoxes in the Lounge.* The synoptic picture of lounges is rich and complex, and presents several contradictions. We close our book by highlighting the inherent paradoxes of life in lounges. The various modes of inquiry of our study permitted us to uncover these inner tensions. Taking up the themes of our study and the paradoxes that emerge from it, we have come up with a conceptualization of two dimensions: the individual and the milieu. This framework is presented in a chart which has the potential to generate further research on teachers' lounges.

# CHAPTER 1

# Modes of Inquiry

We view teachers' lives in schools as highly complex and multifaceted, with the lounge as one component in this complexity. We made two deliberate decisions: First, we decided to gain insights into the lounge environment by using a variety of modes of inquiry, which enabled us to tackle our subject from different and complementary perspectives. This decision supported our second decision, namely, to view all the material we accumulated as "text," which would then have to be interpreted in different ways. Though stemming from different sources, these interpretations yield a composite and valid portrait of the teachers' lounge, derived from the following ways of inquiry.

## Observations

The organizational features of Israeli schools provided us with a perfect setting for inquiring into the various aspects of life in teachers' lounges, the room where teachers were apt to spend significant chunks of their time in school. We started our study with extended periods of observations in different schools in order to get a sense of the environment in which teachers interact during breaks or free periods. We view this physical environment as having a potential impact on their perceptions and feelings concerning their lounges (see appendix I).

Altogether, twenty-six different lounges in high schools were observed by us and by a study group of ten graduate students who served as research assistants. Each lounge was visited three or four times and was observed on each occasion during all breaks and free periods. During the visits to the lounges, sketches and photographs of the physical environment were prepared focusing on external features, such as the arrangement of tables and chairs, as well as the use of the walls as communication channels between school administration and teachers.

Through the videotaping of a full day in a teachers' lounge in one high school, we created a record of the professional and social life there, including the talk, the sounds of voices, the rhythm of movements, and the ebb and flow of groups forming and dispersing. The videotape and the recorded observations constitute texts which are analyzed and presented in different chapters of this book.

Throughout our study we were sensitive and attentive to the voices of the major participants in the life of lounges, i.e., teachers and principals. The voice of the teachers is that of adults defining their place within a social organization and working community, in our case, teachers' lounges.

## Interviews

We conducted in-depth interviews with forty teachers and twelve principals who were chosen at random from the teachers and principals in the observed schools. These interviews provided us with insights into how teachers and principals perceive the characteristics of their lounges and their possible impact on school life.

We decided to adopt an additional mode of listening to teachers, assuming that by writing for us in the form of monologues about their experiences they would help us uncover further aspects of life in lounges.

## Monologues

We asked teachers to respond to a call for submitting written monologues concerning their experiences in the teachers' lounge. We assumed that through the monologues written under the heading of "My Life in the Teachers' Lounge," each teacher would be able to express his or her true feelings without the intervention of a researcher. A monologue is an autonomous unit of discourse. It is a complete unit of statements that can be used in order to understand the meanings assigned by the writer to the object related to, in our case "the lounge." Fifty-three monologues were obtained at random as we sent out a "call for monologues" that invited this writing. The response was extensive: It included primary and high school teachers, as well as student teachers. They constituted a separate group of respondents in our study. All the monologues were analyzed and part of this analysis is presented in chapter 5.

### The Questionnaire

A questionnaire composed of two parts was compiled on the basis of the preliminary interviews with teachers:

(A) A list of twenty characteristics of lounges (e.g., "noisy"; "pleasant atmosphere"; "competitive environment"; "lessons are prepared"; "a place to talk with students") was provided. Teachers were asked to indicate on a Likert-type scale the appropriateness of each characteristic as describing their own teachers' lounge (range 1–5; 1 indicating "not true or very seldom true for the teachers' lounge in my school" and 5 indicating "very often true for the teachers' lounge in my school").

(B) Teachers were asked to assess the perceived impact of teachers' lounges on ten school-related domains (e.g., "improving school climate"; "developing interpersonal relationship between teachers"; "developing educational activities"). Responses were on a Likert-type scale (range 1–5; 1 indicating "no impact" and 5 indicating "great impact"). The questionnaire also included an open-ended section in which they were asked to elaborate on some of their experiences in the lounge and to suggest some metaphors they considered appropriate to describe this room (see appendix II).

The structure of teacher responses to part A of the questionnaire was first examined by employing a factor analysis based on principal components and a varimax rotation of extracted factors. The factor analysis provides a useful and concise summary of responses to individual items, clustered in meaningful groups (factors) based on the pattern of item interrelations.

Factor analysis was also employed in part B of the questionnaire, which focused on perceived spheres of the influence of lounges on school life. The emerging scale was correlated with the factors of lounge characteristics in order to establish a link between the perceived functions of these rooms and the amount of influence teachers attribute to their particular lounge.

Four hundred and nine elementary school teachers (95 percent female) responded to the questionnaire. Most of the teachers were from urban schools (84 percent) and had a mean of twelve years (SD = 7.7) of teaching experience and a mean of seven years (SD = 5.6) in their current school. On average, they reported five workdays per week (SD = 1) and visited their lounges more than twice a day (SD = 1). The time that teachers actually spent in the lounge exceeded one hour (three recesses), and whenever they had an unscheduled free period. The data collected for this part of our study was one component in a larger survey conducted in nineteen elementary schools in Israel, thus providing us with an opportunity to expand our study in additional ways.

The nineteen elementary schools were part of a statewide testing endeavor in math and reading comprehension of elementary students. Data on students' academic achievement in two standard tests, one in math and one in reading comprehension, were collected for each school in the study, aggregated to the school level. These tests had been administered by the Ministry of Education in grades 3 and 5 in all elementary schools in Israel. Based on test results the nineteen schools in our study were divided into two groups: low-achieving and high-achieving, according to their place below or above the average test score. Because the correlation between math and reading test scores was about .9, the results were averaged across the two subjects. In low-achievement schools (8 schools, 181 teachers), the average failure rate was 42 percent, while in high achievement schools (11 schools, 228 teachers), the average failure rate was 14 percent. The two groups of schools were quite comparable with respect to size, teacher-to-student ratio, as well as physical characteristics such as relative classroom space (from total school space) and space per student.

We investigated the patterns of teachers' perception of their lounges in low- versus high-achievement schools.

Two empirical questions guided our data analysis in this section:

1. Are there differences between the teachers in low- and high-achievement schools regarding their perceptions of the teachers' lounge functions?
2. How do teachers in low- and in high-achievement schools associate the teachers' lounge functions with specific domains of influence on school life?

In order to answer the first question, we compared the mean scores of the three lounge functions, and the influence scale, between the two groups of teachers.

To further address the question of links between the perceived functions of teachers' lounges and their influence on school life, we calculated for teachers in low- and in high-achievement schools, separately, correlation between each function score, and the ten items describing specific domains of influence. Although individual items reflect a general influence factor, it was considered especially important to go into such level of detail in order to shed more light on differences between low- versus high-achievement schools.

Our analysis of the questionnaires was based on accepted statistical procedures which provided us with the basis for our emerging concepts concerning life in the teachers' lounge on the one hand, and on the other, the relationship between events in the lounge and in the classroom.

## The Notion of Text and its Uses

The intention of integrating different modes of inquiry and orientations in our study led us to refer to the variety of sources for our data as text. A text has to be interpreted in order to get a sense of the inherent nature of an event, discourse, or character. We were interested in gaining insights into the nature of the teachers' lounge. In other words, our methodological approach is based on the interpretative paradigm.

Our aim is to direct and concentrate the attention of the reader to specific events, objects, ideas, and interactions within the lounge. Analyzing the varied texts from many perspectives serves the process of creating knowledge which emerges from the composition of all these perspectives.

Text is a concept easier to characterize than to define. Usually the concept text means the written words: a group of sentences which, when put together, serves to express an idea. We can also refer to text in a wider meaning, based on the distinction between the common notion of text that we have just mentioned, and the theatrical text. The theatrical text has a wider meaning. Thus the distinction will be formulated as follows: "the world created through words will be called *the theatrical text, i.e., the performance of a play, the production, as opposed to the written literary text*" (Schonmann 1995, p. 176).

For the purpose of the analysis in the following chapters, we will refer to the teachers' lounge as a place in which multiple texts originate. We give meaning to the texts through our interpretations and thus create a multifaceted portrait of life in lounges. Giving interpretation to text is the art of applying one's frame of reference as opposed to directly participating in the events. Interpretation is an act everyone is involved in while dealing with text. "It is the way of adding, or subtracting from a direct communication" (Spolin 1973, p. 384). It is the essence of any analysis which aims to give meaning to data. In his book, *Is There a Text in This Class*, Stanley Fish described the mental processes we employ while reading text. He claims: "The place where sense is made or not made is the reader's mind rather than the printed page or the space between the covers of the book" (Fish 1980, p. 21).

Interpretation can be made from several points of view. When analyzing text from a dramatic point of view we employ dramatic concepts, such as "dramatic tension," "conventions," "the fourth wall," "catharsis," "time and timing," "place and space"; these are all elements which help give meaning to the experience in the teachers' lounge and are elaborated in the relevant chapters in this book. The researcher's work is to find the reality beyond the text and to help the reader understand the narrator's perspective.

## Our Role as Researchers

The "fourth wall" is a theatre convention that facilitates the suspension of disbelief, and contributes to the make-believe world of the play. In her book, *Welcome to the Theatre*, Boyce (1987) indicates that,

> The stage is enclosed on three sides, which often constitute the walls of the set, in which there are doors and windows. The fourth wall is an invisible barrier through which the audience views the play. Originally, in plays performed on a proscenium stage, the performers did not acknowledge the presence of the audience. The play progressed while the audience eavesdropped on the performance via the invisible fourth wall. This provided a separation of audience and actor that was thought to be desirable. This fourth wall concept provided a psychological barrier helpful to both the actor and audience. (p. 22)

The convention of the "fourth wall" allows the audience to feel like unseen observers who watch the events on the stage as if they were part of reality. When the illusion of reality is achieved, the spectators tend to feel great empathy toward the figures on the stage.

We borrowed the "fourth wall" convention for our inquiry as one mode of observation, which gave us the advantage of feeling that we were "seeing but not being seen." We watched, listened, and noted our impressions. After a while, we felt a need to take part in the situation. We continued to follow the concept of the "fourth wall," but now played the role of an active audience by introducing our video camera into the teachers' lounge. At the start, the result of our interference in the flow of teachers' lives in their collective private room caused tense acting and behavior, but this happened only at the beginning. After a while, when the teachers got used to us and lost interest in our presence, it became possible to peep through the "fourth wall" while being fully aware that there were boundaries between actors, namely the teachers, and the audience, ourselves, the researchers. The boundaries were well understood albeit invisible, and encouraged us as the audience to limit our participation in the process we observed, and to behave as if we were spectators at a play.

Everybody knew about us and we knew about them, but the events in the lounge continued without our active input. Sometimes we felt a strong desire to join in or to speak to the teachers, but at this stage of our observations we agreed to keep to the "fourth wall" convention and stay as silent observers only. We were observers in the sense of watching a play. In *Hamlet*, for example, when some viewers reach the scene where Polonius is hiding behind the curtains, they often feel a strong desire to shout out and warn both of them, "Beware, Polonius!" or, "Hamlet, don't do it; it's Polonius—not the king." To do so, of course, would destroy the illusion for the rest of the audience and, as a spectator, one must not lose sight of the convention which keeps us at a distance.

## Concluding Comments

In spite of the localized context of our study, we invite the reader to examine the insights gained concerning teacher development and communities of adults in schools. This first chapter introduces the reader to our research paradigm, its substantive and syntactic structure. The life in teachers' lounges is perceived as a text to be decoded and interpreted. The notion of text played out in the lounge led us to employ dramatic concepts, such as "conventions" and "catharsis," which help us give meaning to the experiences in teachers' lounges. We found the "fourth wall" convention useful for describing our own role as researchers: feeling, seeing but not seen, like spectators at a play. We were intrigued by the teachers' own perceptions of their lounges and employed a variety of research methods to gain insights into these perceptions. Though we saw the lounge as a separate niche in the culture of schools, we were interested in the possible relationships between life in the lounge and the teaching and learning taking place in classrooms. Therefore, we investigated the patterns of teachers' perceptions of their lounges in the low- versus high-achievement schools that had participated in statewide tests in math and reading.

The various modes of inquiry led us to observe teachers' lounges as a place in which a subculture is created. We agree with Bruner who showed that education is a "complex pursuit of fitting a culture to the needs of its members and of fitting its members and their ways of knowing to the needs of the culture" (Bruner 1996, p. 43).

In the following chapters we would like to share and discuss these ways of viewing and thinking about how teachers create their own subculture to fit their social and professional knowledge.

# CHAPTER 2

# Social Situations

Studying life in classrooms raises several questions concerning the social situation developing in this environment: Is the myth of the lonely teacher still valid? Which elements constitute the social situation in the lounge? What norms are reflected in teachers' interactions in the lounge? We will attempt to propose some answers to these questions, starting with the myth of the lonely teacher.

## The Myth of the Lonely Teacher

The inside stories of lounges, revealing norms of discourse and behavior, friendships and power struggles, and tense as well as relaxed moments, constitute the social situation of lounges. Viewing the social situations as an essential component of the professional lives of teachers, we challenge the widespread notion that teaching is a lonely profession. This idea has survived more than three decades (Jackson 1968; Lortie 1975; Dreeben 1970).

Our basic assumption is that teachers' lounges constitute a unique territory in the educational environment of schools. By its definition the lounge belongs to the teachers, and the activities that occur within its walls reflect the links between them. On the basis of this assumption we argue against some of Lortie's statements in *Schoolteacher* (1975):

> Relationships with other adults do not stand at the heart of teachers' psychological world. (p. 187)

Although Lortie was aware of the complex relationships among teachers, he did not examine the teachers' lounge, which we believe is a central site for deciphering these relationships. While trying to avoid simplification of describing teachers in either-or terms, he drew the following picture:

> The cellular form of school organization, and the attendant time and space ecology, puts interactions between teachers at the margin of their daily work. Individualism characterizes their socialization . . . It seems that teachers can work effectively without the active assistance of colleagues, since teacher-teacher interaction does not seem to play a critical part in the work life of our respondents. (p. 192)

Lortie claimed that being shaped by deeper commitments to students, the relationships teachers have with other adults are secondary, and derivative in nature. Goodlad and Klein (1970) made a similar claim:

> It would appear that teachers are very much alone in their work. It is not just a matter of being alone, all alone with children in a classroom cell, although this is a significant part of their aloneness. Rather, it is the feeling and in large measure the actuality—of not being supported by someone who knows about their work, who is sympathetic to it, who wants to help and, indeed, does help. This is, in part, an unhappy consequence of the inviolate status of the classroom and the assumed autonomy of the teacher in it. This aloneness becomes poignant in the face of problems which, clearly, cannot be solved by the individual teacher alone. (pp. 93–94)

It is possible that for many teachers the loneliness in their classroom overshadows any social interactions in the teachers' lounge. We are aware of the wide diversity among schools at different age levels and in different cultures in which these descriptions might be valid. Still, we question these suppositions by asking whether this description of the characteristics of the profession in the 1970s is still accurate and holds in the reality of school culture nowadays with its growing emphasis on professional communities of teachers? We examine this question by investigating teachers' relationships with peers as reflected in social situations in teachers' lounges.

## The Social Actions

The situations in teachers' lounges are communicative by their nature. They are social phenomena, structured in the context of time, place, and the involved participants, the teachers. An important term for understanding the social situation of lounges is Weber's (1968) term "social action." The importance of the term lies in the understanding that human actions are deliberate. Actions are not automatic or accidental but express the ability of persons to grasp their environment and act in a reasonable and planned way, based on their interpretations.

The social actions of teachers in their lounges have not been widely explored as yet, though scholars such as Lieberman & Miller (1984) mention the lounge as a site for social and professional interactions with colleagues. Such rooms are part of the social reality of teachers (Hargreaves & Woods 1984). For instance, in the chapter on the meaning of staffroom humor, Woods argues that this is a major way in which teachers

> come to terms with their job and reconcile their selves with the demands of the teacher role. (Hargreaves & Woods, 1984, p. 190)

And, in his chapter on staffroom news, Hammersley (1984) looks at certain features of the occupational culture of teaching as revealed in staffroom talk. He views staffroom news as

> A kind of collective stocktaking in which teachers compare notes and bring themselves up to date

> about the pupils whom they all face in the classroom. (p. 212)

According to Hammersley, teachers' exchanges also serve a rhetorical function:

> They seem to be designed to protect the teachers' professional identities in the face of the threat to their sense of their own competence posed by the behaviour of the pupils. (p. 212)

A study conducted by Keinan (1994) showed that in their staffroom, teachers represent their own professional culture to each other. After analyzing teachers' talk in the staffroom, Keinan concluded that the meaning of professionalism in teaching is based on a sense of educational commitment.

The opportunities for interactions with peers provided by teachers' lounges are extremely important for counteracting the sense of being unsupported, and alone. The teachers' lounge is the only unit in the school in which it is possible to examine events from the point of view of teachers being together. The very fact of occupying a place in the teachers' lounge as part of a collective being transforms teachers there into an entity which can be characterized in terms of the lounge community. The community is conceived by its members, and by the students and their parents, as one group. This kind of being "together" can be contrasted with the separate contexts of the cellular structure of classes, to and from which teachers come and go with the ringing of the bell.

The social situation in lounges is shaped by a basic element. In this situation pure privacy does not exist, the teacher is forced to "take a role" and to play a part in the public situation which is a social one by its nature. The blurring of boundaries between the public and private spheres, discussed in chapter 4, is based on an approach which emphasizes the duality in the nature of any social reality.

Accepting the notion that social actions are to be understood as expressing the ability of persons to grasp their environment and to interpret it, we focus on the observable occurrences in lounges, the social facts which may be perceived as the building blocks of social actions.

Social facts help describe the social situation of teachers' lounges, as well as of classrooms. Shapiro & Ben-Eliezer (1991) explain a classroom situation in terms of social facts: i.e., students are sitting; the teacher is standing; the teacher asks questions; students answer; students who wish to speak raise their hands. The classroom is described as a well-defined place where activities planned beforehand are carried out. In the frame of these activities some of the participants are called "students." Their freedom of action is limited by a set of clearly defined rules which permit or prohibit certain behaviors.

Social facts, as Shapiro & Ben-Eliezer (1991) argue, shape the identity of classes which might be described as places in which teacher and students are partners in the same social entity. Classes differ from each other by the specific way their inhabitants behave. According to Shapiro & Ben-Eliezer, some classes are characterized by bad manners in the acting out of social facts, such as speaking without permission or making a lot of noise, while other classes are highly disciplined. Still, the notion of social facts applies to all classes. This concept of "social fact" might be applied as well to teachers' lounges: teachers come in, read the information presented on the notice boards, check their mail boxes, prepare coffee for themselves. Students are not allowed in. The sound of the bell is the sign to stop or to begin any action.

Like classrooms, teachers' lounges might differ in the manner in which their inhabitants express these "social facts," thus creating very different lounge climates. The social situation of lounges is a blend of observable events which can be traced, and in which one can participate. Hidden from the public eye, hard to define events are also part of the life in lounges, and are often the cause for individuals to detach themselves from the group, feeling uncomfortable and uneasy. The idea of covert events leads us to a discussion of the inner grammar of the teachers' lounges, which encompasses both overt and covert elements.

## The Inner Grammar

The social situation of life in teachers' lounges might be conceived of as a text. Like written texts characterized by their syntax, the social text of lounges might be understood in terms of its inner grammar which creates a special syntax. Some features of this inner grammar are overt and directly observable, such as the social facts and actions mentioned above. Other structures of the inner grammar are conventions and norms which are covert, yet implicit in the observable social actions.

The events in teachers' lounges become meaningful, and sometimes even predictable, when the situation is structured, when there is a common basis for the perception and interpretation of these events, or when there are regular patterns of behaviors or roles. Common and routine events in the lounge, such as providing information about a student, or an upcoming lecture, become part of the common basis for interpretation, and their meaning is easily shared among all participants in the social situation.

Sometimes, however, the events in the teachers' lounge are unusual, unique, and the individual interpretation of the situation is not part of the general, accepted basis for interpretation. The social actions in the teachers' lounge develop into routine patterns of behavior, which constitute one part of the inner grammar of teachers' lounges and serve to define collegial norms. Unique situations are conceived as another part of the inner grammar of teachers' lounges, and will be defined as dramatic and "tension" situations. The development and outcomes of such situations are uncertain: they are open-ended and unpredictable. The framework of the "inner grammar" of teachers' lounges allows us to explain what happens when a tense situation is resolved and teachers are able to return to their routines.

We shall turn now to some of the implicit structures of the inner grammar of lounges as expressed in the following norms: a) **norms of collegiality** b) **norms of the "good colleague."**

## Norms of Collegiality

Norms of collegiality were examined carefully by Little (1982, 1990). The term **collegiality** has remained conceptually amorphous and ideologically sanguine as Little claimed,

> Advocates have imbued it with a sense of virtue—the expectation that any interaction that breaks the isolation of teachers will contribute in some fashion to the knowledge, skill, judgment or commitment that individuals bring to their work and will enhance the collective capacity of groups or institutions. (1990 p. 509)

An interesting synonym to collegiality is offered by Cunningham & Gresso (1993) who claimed that

> An appropriate synonym for collegiality is community. When people have a sense of community, they belong, and have pride in the group . . . Some of the characteristics of a collegial group are honesty, trust, loyalty, commitment, caring . . . Collegiality is characterized by the amount of open and honest interaction within the group and a clear and quick understanding of what group members are saying . . . Collegiality exists when each member feels free and encouraged to participate, and when members feel that they share equally in influencing the group. (pp. 99–100)

The ability of members of a community to understand each other clearly and quickly is linked to a set of shared norms which develop over time as exemplified in the following vignette in which Shapiro & Ben-Eliezer (1991) suggest that we imagine a group of friends who decide to gather every Friday afternoon in the municipal park to play football. After a few meetings, which go very well, one of the group decides to surprise his friends and brings soft drinks. The friends like this idea very much, and the boy who prior to this was quiet and not outstanding in any way becomes prominent and, for the first time, is even nominated to be the organizer of the team. The boy continues to bring soft drinks every Friday until once he is forced to stay longer at work and is unable to bring the expected drinks with him. In spite of his delay he comes finally to the park. To his surprise, his friends are hostile toward him, and a few of them even call him names. This story serves as a starting point to our discussion because it illustrates very clearly the paradigm of a "norm": What is expected? From whom? What is acceptable? What is not acceptable? What are the possible results of our actions?

The norms of teachers' lounges are created during the daily interaction between teachers. Norms which concern ways of speaking, of dressing, and ways to conduct routine activities, might be perceived as "collegial norms." People who have a group relationship tend to reach an agreement in areas relevant to the interactions in this group. Norms can be implicit, and hard to identify. The more explicit the norms, the easier it is for new members to enter a group and adapt to its ways. The view of norms as unwritten rules and as expectations to behave in a certain manner, provides an explanatory framework for some of the dilemmas, dramas, and tensions which can arise in lounges, and which are presented in the following sections.

Life of teachers in school might cause behaviors which contradict acceptable norms. For example, according to the normative perception acceptable in teachers' lounges, students are not allowed to enter this area. When students do enter the lounge because a teacher has invited them, it constitutes a breaking of norms. Thus a dilemma situation is created. On the one hand, a teacher has clearly acted in a manner which caused an unusual, unexpected tension situation to arise, in contradiction to the expected "collegial norms" of the inner grammar of the lounge. On the other hand, another important school norm concerns the role of teachers as helping their students. Dilemmas in the lounge can be caused by contrary expectations for behavior. For instance, in the lounge teachers might all talk at the same time, while in their classes a strict order of speaking might be adhered to. Some teachers might find this situation highly stressful, reacting verbally and trying to stop the racket.

Since life in teachers' lounges reflects the culture of collegial norms, it is important for inhabitants of this culture to understand the nature of these norms. Two events exemplify the role norms of collegiality play in the social situation of teachers' lounges.

## Giving up a Free Day

In one teachers' lounge in a senior highschool, a group of six English teachers who were very close friends, used to eat breakfast together every Tuesday. That was their way of showing cohesiveness as a professional group. It became a ritual which involved bringing coffee and cake, telling jokes, and creating their own unique atmosphere. One morning, the principal told one of the teachers that her schedule had been changed, and that in the future Tuesday would be her day off. The teacher told the principal that it was impossible for her to change days because Tuesday was the day she met with her group of English teachers to discuss work in an informal meeting. She wanted to continue to participate in these meetings, and was willing to give up her day off for the sake of not withdrawing from the group in which she was a member. Her interpretation of norms of collegiality meant spending a morning together with her colleagues every Tuesday.

## Breaking the Norm

Collegial norms might be considered by some members of the group to be most unpleasant even though the term itself has a positive connotation. Norms are behaviors which are implicitly accepted by a group of people, and any deviation from these norms might be understood as a critique and an attempt to change the norm. Eating in the teachers' lounge is one of the more obvious norms that exist. Teachers' routines, that is, their choice of companions, the way they prepare their coffee, all reflect these norms. Tammy, for example, had many negative experiences to impart about the teachers' lounge. She disliked the noise there, as well as the messiness. She told us that she had tried to bring pots of flowers to decorate the room but no one had paid any attention. She became upset because other teachers left their dirty glasses, bread crumbs, and dirty ashtrays on the table. Above all she was upset with the fact that she could not change these norms of behavior. She stopped entering the teachers' lounge, except to get her mail or read the announcements. However, since she broke the norm of being part of the group she sensed that she could not stay there. At the end of the year she moved to another school.

Misunderstandings, conflicts, and unpleasantness in the lounge can be explained on the basis of cultural and individual differences concerning the norms of using time and space (Hall 1959). A new teacher, for example, might enter the lounge and sit on a "free" chair without knowing that this space was usually occupied by one of the senior teachers. The new teacher might feel uneasy, without understanding the "hostility" around him or her.

Another common situation, concerning the norms of time use in the lounge, arises when the bell rings after a break. The ringing is a sign to return to classrooms, but some teachers might tend to delay their exit from the lounge. Teachers who leave the lounge with the first sound of the bell break a collegial norm, and might become the object of jokes, or even hostile remarks.

Collegial norms of accepted behavior in the lounge are usually shared by staff and students alike. Thus, students know whether the lounge is out-of-bounds or not, when and under what circumstances they are allowed to enter it. Any unusual behavior tends to create a tense atmosphere. The following is an example of such a situation:

> Mary, a seventeen-year-old student, entered the lounge one day, and kissed and hugged her teacher. The other teachers who were there were unable to accept this as a normative way of behaving and expressed their dissatisfaction. They did not know that Mary had been seriously ill. She had returned to school after being treated for cancer for a long period. Esther, the teacher, was extremely pleased to see Mary, and showed her delight. She could not tell her friends the reasons for the affectionate behavior because Mary's family had asked [that] the illness be kept a secret.

## Norms of a "Good Colleague"

Beyond the norms of collegiality, i.e., those norms which determine the kind of behavior acceptable in the lounge, one might find norms concerning the behavior of a "good colleague," someone who has a positive impact on our professional lives. Norms of a "good colleague" are perceived by us to be the basis for productive professional communities. Beyond the sharing of common norms, communities of teachers might develop a notion of what it means to be a "good colleague," something to strive for in a continuous process of growth.

A brief example should clarify the nature of this term. Imagine three elementary school teachers who had different reasons to become teachers. The first teacher chose the profession in the belief that teaching is a very important social function. The second did so because she considered it a suitable job for a working mother. The third chose teaching because of the social status of being a teacher, as well as the possibility of upward social mobility. Each of these teachers would have a different view of the impact of a "good colleague" on their lives. For the teacher motivated by the status of being a teacher, a good colleague might be someone who provided her with a sense of belonging to the professional community, someone, for example, who would invite her to join an informal discussion in the lounge. For the woman who chose teaching because of its suitability for mothers, a good colleague might be someone who would substitute for her in case of a child's illness. The teacher who chose teaching because she considered education important, would probably have professional criteria for a "good colleague," such as a readiness to share professional knowledge. These are only hypothetical cases presented as examples of the various ways of perceiving the nature of good colleagues.

What then is the norm of a "good colleague"? From our interviews with teachers, it became clear that in Israel *Firgun* is a central element in the concept of a "good colleague." *Firgun* is a term in Hebrew that expresses lack of envy for the success of others. In teaching, this means the kind of relationship which serves to advance a good professional reputation. The good colleague is one who is not jealous of the successes of colleagues but, on the contrary, helps to further their reputation. This matter is of great importance, according to our interviews, and is considered by teachers as more important than helping to prepare materials for a lesson, or helping to solve a problem. *Firgun* is central and basic to the perception of a "good colleague." How can we understand this phenomenon? It is a process in which one praises a colleague and gives him or her one's full support. It is a social action which influences professional work. A teacher's work is influenced by the way colleagues can advance one another's reputation. This is one factor in the creation of social cohesion in the teaching community.

Social cohesion—*Gibush*—has a great value in the life of Israeli teachers. It can be understood in the framework of Katriel & Nesher (1986) and Katriel (1991) who studied this social aspect in Israeli schools. They found that one of the major concerns of every teacher is to create a cohesive atmosphere in the class. The same perception of good and cohesive interpersonal relationships is transferred into the culture of lounges, and shapes the norm of a good colleague. Though the concepts of *Firgun* and *Gibush* are terms which have emerged in the Israeli culture, they might be meaningful in other cultures of teaching as well, as they relate to some of the basic concerns of the profession. The main point we wish to make is that teachers are part of a professional community, even when they are in the confines of their classrooms. They care about other teachers and they are also concerned about their own professional image.

It is important to note that the "good colleague" is not necessarily an unidimensional concept. As argued at the beginning of this section, different teachers might create their own notion of a "good colleague." Still, it seems that in Israeli culture, features of mutual support, leading to social cohesiveness, are perceived as desirable qualities.

Teachers' stories presented below reveal how the cohesive situations in lounges might create an atmosphere of mutual support. Novice teachers, however, might find it difficult to become part of a cohesive group as shown by the following anecdote.

## A Novice Teacher

Mary's story reveals how important the sense of social cohesion is for teachers, and how it can lead to a sense of support, the sense of having others rejoice with you in your successes.

> When Mary was a new teacher in school, and did not yet feel "one of the group," she used to stand for a long time preparing her coffee, waiting for the bell to rescue her from the feeling of being alone and isolated, giving her the excuse to return to her class where she felt she belonged. Later, however, when she became a more experienced teacher, she began to appreciate the comfort of the teachers' lounge; then she found she was waiting for the bell to ring to end the lesson, so she could go to the lounge. She felt she was part of the group, which had accepted her and was ready to share work experiences with her in a supportive way. She wanted to take part in this social process; she felt

a strong desire to enter the teachers' lounge to spend time with her friends.

### A Sick Colleague

Sometimes the social cohesion has far-reaching results.

> Thelma, a senior teacher in a middle school told us about a teacher with cancer who was consequently forced to give up work. For more than eighteen months the teachers in her school took care of her. They visited her, cooked for her, and cleaned her apartment until her last day. All this work was organized in meetings in the teachers' lounge. There were daily meetings where teachers exchanged information and shared their feelings. As time passed, the number of teachers who wanted to be involved increased. "It strengthened us and made us more cohesive. It is a pity that we know how to get together when there is a problem and that we don't do it on regular days." These words express a wide notion shared among teachers. Thelma expressed a strong desire to learn from this special situation. She said: "We were very good colleagues; I hope we can continue to be good colleagues."

### Saving the Social Cohesiveness of the Lounge

In cases which threaten to weaken the social cohesion of a lounge, one of the teachers might decide to take action. Nira's story is an example of such a situation.

> A conflict between two teachers gave rise to increasing quarrels in the presence of the other teachers in the lounge. Only the bell released them from the embarrassment and humiliation [of] being involved in a public feud. Nira thought it was disgraceful, regardless of who was responsible: she organized the teach-

ers in the lounge to decide that the two teachers should not enter the lounge until they had apologize to each other in front of their colleagues. One of the teachers did apologize willingly because he felt uneasy about the whole situation but the other refused to do so. The area of misunderstanding widened, and the second teacher was forced to leave the school at the end of the year.

## Concluding Comments

Life in teachers' lounges encompasses more than observable, routine actions of people relaxing in their own territory, drinking coffee, and chatting with colleagues. Beyond these aspects, one might find in the social situations of the lounge expressions of norms and collegiality and unexpected moments of dramatic tension.

Questioning the myth of the lonely teacher led us to investigate the interconnectedness of teachers and the social events in their lounges. In our analysis, we deciphered the inner grammar of social situations in lounges by employing the concepts of collegiality, the "good colleague," support, and cohesion, *Firgun* and *Gibush*. Cunningham & Gresso (1993) emphasize that

> Collegiality is the basis for group spirit and the bonds that hold a group together, allowing it to achieve extraordinary success. Once team spirit develops, the power of the team will work in almost any situation. (p. 111)

The phenomenon of a "good colleague" seems to us a crucial component in our understanding of the nature of teachers' communities, but it has not yet received much attention in the literature. In different schools and cultures, the norms of a "good colleague" might develop in divergent ways, leading to different results for the nature of teachers' communities in these schools. Our approach to life in lounges as a text to be deciphered led us to the notion of the "inner grammar," with its two different kinds of features, i.e., those which are directly observable, and those which are covert and implicit, open to diverse interpretations. Since we view the culture of lounges to be strongly interrelated with the general professional climate of schools, we believe in the necessity of striving for insights into the "inner grammar" of teachers' lounges.

This chapter has highlighted some of the positive experiences of teachers in their community. In our attempts to gain a comprehensive understanding of the complex nature of events in the lounge, we turn next to a dramatic perspective that aided us in deciphering the "inner grammar" of the tensions, struggles, and dilemmas faced by teachers.

# CHAPTER 3

# Dramatic Language

How can dramatic concepts enrich our understanding of the interaction in lounges? In what ways does the dramatic concept of "conventions" extend our understanding of the norms of lounges? Does "catharsis" as a dramatic concept shed new light on the social cohesiveness in lounges and its function in the development of a community of teachers?

We tend to think that regarding teachers as "actors" in their classrooms might be counterproductive to authentic teaching. Who then are the spectators, if any? Are students also actors in an unfolding play? Who is supposed to author the script? And most important, when does the play end and reflection about it begin? Therefore, instead of viewing the teacher as an actor in the classroom, or lounge, as if in a play, we suggest using certain dramatic frameworks that might enhance our ability to interpret educational phenomena, without forcing a rigid structure on them.

What we have tried to do is to use the language of drama and theatre in order to expand the range of tools with which we can conduct a social analysis of the professional lives of teachers and understand some of the events which take place in the staffroom.

## The Uses of Dramatic Terms

Interaction between people, perception of time, and a defined place are the three main components defining communication in lounges; they are also the three major components defining communication in drama. Understanding their inner grammar leads to a set of conventions and to the concept of collective catharsis which lie at the core of the culture of lounges. Conventions and catharsis are used in this chapter to reveal emotional aspects of the mood and atmosphere created in lounges through interpersonal interactions.

Whereas in this chapter we focus on interactions between people in terms of conventions and catharsis, in the next chapter we shall concentrate on dramatic perceptions of "time" and "place." The importance of using theatrical terms for analysis of events in lounges is that these terms address dynamic processes and through this emphasis direct us toward possibilities of change in patterns of relationships.

Drama, by definition, is a series of unexpected and surprising events occurring in social situations in which people experience some confrontation or struggle. In fact, drama is present wherever people live. It is customary to use the term as a metaphor, such as "a drama in the family" or "a drama in the life of a country." Drama in this context refers to those events which are parallel to forms of drama in theatre in that they involve the participants in the event in highly stimulating situations. Intuitively we understand the meaning of "a tragedy in the family," or its opposite, "this is a comedy." Comedy and tragedy are, in fact, the genres that define drama as a series of events, including elements such as emotional tension, excitement, and unexpected shifts of emphasis. Likewise we conceive of life in lounges as composed of sets of dramatic elements.

Just as theatre and drama have evolved from life itself, we argue that using dramatic and theatrical terms enables us to define and interpret social situations that happen in real life.

The sources of the dramatic approach to research the life of people and society are dramatic terms found in the works of modern theoreticians in the fields of psychology and sociology. Among the most prominent are Freud, Mead, and Goffman, Harre and Lyman & Scott.

For Freud, and for Mead (1934), the mind and soul are regarded as the site where dramatic processes take place. According to Lyman & Scott (1975), the dramatic orientation elaborated on in Freud's work is apparent in almost every aspect of his theory. Some of his basic terminology such as the *Oedipus complex*, the *Electra complex*, and *Catharsis* are drawn from Greek tragedy. The mental lives according to Freud are a kind of drama performed on three different levels: the unconscious, the subconscious and the conscious. The drama is activated by the id, the ego, and the super-ego.

For Goffman (1959), we find that the main issue in a person's life is dealing with the self. Every man represents himself in everyday life so that he can obtain most of what he wishes. Every man carries a persona that aims at exposing the self according to the specific situation that he encounters. Goffman explains that personification is the basis for any social situation. There is no doubt that making sense of life situations cannot be reduced only to metaphors provided by the theatre. But examining the self and society from a theatrical perspective provides theoreticians with a framework to understand people and their world.

Turner (1976) developed the concept of social drama which might help us gain such an understanding. Social dramas, according to Turner, constitute

> our native way of manifesting ourselves to ourselves and, of declaring where power and meaning lie and how they are distributed. (p. 78)

Turner regards the social drama

> as a process of converting particular values and ends, distributed over a range of actors, into a system (which is always temporary and provisional) of shared or consensual meaning. (p. 75)

Consensual meanings might reveal themselves in conventions.

## Conventions

While social norms, such as that of collegiality or that of a "good colleague" are associated with moral values, conventions do not necessarily have value connotations, though sometimes they may not be free of them. Conventions, in the dramatic framework, express the readiness to name and accept a certain phenomenon and thus the actor and the spectator are able to act accordingly. Conventions are based upon conduct and manners dictated in advance that have been absorbed by the audience of a specific culture (Rap, 1973, p. 121). The central convention in theatre could be, for instance, "an agreement to pretend." According to that convention, the audience, as well as the artists in the theatre, are both willing to accept the convention that one must refer, for example, to an artificial sign as though it were a natural sign. Therefore a white actor who is made up with black paint playing the part of Othello, must be treated as a black Moor without ever questioning his white complexion. In the theatre, contrary to real life, one can break the rules of nature and turn them into conventions. Thus, one can hang a cardboard picture on a wall and claim it is the sun. However, it is impossible to "break" those rules that refer to the interaction of codes of conduct among people, because the rules of conduct practiced in their everyday lives are the rules practiced on the stage. This must be the basis of understanding conventions, as well as comprehending the implications for teachers' lounges which are derived from that framework.

There exists a primary agreement and a basic understanding that a school is a social institute with responsibility for all that occurs within its grounds. The teachers' lounge is part of the working environment in the context of an educational institute. Teachers are expected to arrive at a mutual understanding with their colleagues over the means of dealing with the set of normative prohibitions and demands found in the lounge. Certain conventions are part of this institution. For instance, though the lounge is noisy and crowded, it is defined as a place of rest. The naming of the lounge as a place of rest allows all participants to agree to "pretend" that in spite of the noise, and even the work that is sometimes carried out there, the lounge is indeed a place of rest for the teacher. Norms of behavior representing rest or, conversely, work, may coexist, and even complement each other, in the agreed-upon convention of accepting the room as a place of rest.

Humor in the lounge is another example of a convention, in that what is accepted as an object of laughter is specific to the lounge. For instance, there exists an unwritten agreement among teachers there, not "to see" the faults or mistakes of their colleagues or to make them the object of jokes. Meeting daily in the teachers' room maintains an unwritten code of behavior, and defines boundaries of partnership existing among the teachers. Conventions are therefore related to a collective obligation, and a solidarity created by the teachers among themselves. Solidarity might become a convention in the teachers' lounge. Solidarity as a dynamic process in the lounge is another way of viewing the function of support (*Firgun*) and social cohesion (*Gibush*) discussed above. The case of the sick colleague provides a good example of solidarity among teachers who feel mutually responsible for each other. Nurturing solidarity is based upon the need of teachers to construct a sort of a "safety belt" for themselves in their world.

## Dramatic Action

Conventions are expressed in the presentation of actions and behaviors. The concept of dramatic action might help us to understand the process of expressing conventions. Burgess & Gaudy (1986) state that,

> dramatic actions are the concrete, physical expression of role; they give dramatic form to abstract thoughts and feelings and are therefore symbolic and meaningful. (p. 31)

Dramatic actions fulfill different functions. O'Toole (1992) speaks about three functions at least:

> What it denotes for the enactor, the **purposive** function, relates to the tasks that form the basis of the action. What it denotes for others, the **communicative** function, relates to the constructions to be put upon the action by others. The action is also necessarily **expressive**, where the action reveals aspects of the character's nature that modify or throw light on the purposes and may permit renegotiation of details of character and relationship within the drama. (p. 40)

These functions can be perceived in the actions of teachers in their lounge. A novice teacher who feels uncomfortable in the lounge, an 'outsider' in the community of teachers, might be observed pouring herself a cup of coffee and drinking it quickly while standing near the coffee pot. The purposive function seems to be clear: the teacher performs an everyday social act and refreshes herself by drinking coffee. The communicative function is more difficult to interpret. How is her action construed by the other teachers? Do they see her as an aloof, asocial person? Do they perceive her action as indicating merely the hurry and pressure of professional duties? This novice teacher's action of drinking coffee has also an expressive function, and might be interpreted as providing insights into deeper and different meanings, revealing her insecurity and feelings of loneliness in the bustling lounge. This renegotiated interpretation might lead others in the lounge to interact with the novice teacher in ways which will serve to make her feel a member of the teachers' community.

There seems to be a certain balance between the routine actions in the lounge, conventions and norms, and the unexpected event which creates dramatic tension. Dramatic tension might be defined according to O'Toole (1992),

> As a set of emotional reactions which percipients of a drama experience individually and as a group. (p. 27)

Like any drama which has its basis in the tension between stasis, the routine and expected components of events, and the disruption of stasis by the unexpected, occurrences in teachers' lounges move between "routine" and "tense" situations.

Incidents in the lounge, creating tense situations and dilemmas, might be accompanied by very intense feelings and emotional outbursts. Such moments of tension might be defused by a process we call "collective catharsis," which will be described in the following section. The distinctive feature of this catharsis is that it is experienced in, and through, communal actions.

## The Nature of "Collective Catharsis"

Social cohesion and norms of collegiality and conventions enable teachers to create an atmosphere conducive to everyday work. Shipman (1986) suggested that all schools manifest a certain amount of conflict due to the fact that they are necessarily restrictive, but all have areas of agreement:

> The conflict focus shows how the backstage is related to the onstage, how subcultures persist and how friction can even be present but not destructive. Staff and pupils not only know the cues and symbols that refer to school life on the surface, but also those that give meaning to the clashes between them. The very existence of schools and their organization create conflicts, but the mechanisms outlined earlier guarantee that even in the worst school some sort of order, however perilous, usually prevails. (p. 90)

From this perspective, Shipman argues that teaching is an

> accommodation to undesirable but inevitable conflicts. (p. 90)

Teachers learn those parts of school life which will lead to either disagreement or to cooperative and enjoyable work. The teachers' lounge can be viewed as a "shelter," a place of refuge from the complex, conflict-laden interaction between staff and students. The metaphor of "shelter" was suggested by the teachers themselves and was brought up constantly throughout the interviews and in the open-ended parts of the questionnaire. This figurative notion was expressed by Yona, an experienced high school teacher:

> The teacher needs to liberate himself from the constant mask he is forced to wear, he has to "let off steam" and behave naturally with friends. When the bell rings for a break the teacher, metaphorically speaking, is absorbed into the teachers' lounge, which becomes a shelter.

The need to "let off steam" gives the teachers' lounge its cathartic role, which is part of its social function.

**The Concept of Catharsis**

Catharsis is a difficult concept in dramatic literature. The term appears originally in chapter 6 of Aristotle's *Poetics*, where it is associated with pity and fear and is clearly related to the effect or the aim of the tragedy's affective power. Vaughn (1978) maintains that the difficulty in interpreting "catharsis" is due in part to the problem of translation, and that each of the many theories of catharsis is based upon a particular translation of the key passage of ten Greek words in the original (pp. 26–27). The well-known way of understanding catharsis is based on the "purgation" theory which suggests that tragedy arouses emotions of pity and fear in the spectators and then purges or eliminates these emotions. One of the many other interpretations of catharsis is "clarification," a concept which does not deny the emotional power of tragedy but sees this power in the plot itself. In other words, through the selecting and ordering processes of art, the incidents of the play are made clear in terms of "probability" and "necessity," and this clarity of action is the source of tragic pleasure (Vaughn, p. 27). Boyce (1987) argues that there is a therapeutic and educational benefit to catharsis (p. 156). If catharsis is to be therapeutic and educational, it must be an experience that is genuinely felt as well as intelligently understood. Excitement is stirred up within the spectators causing them to release a flood of emotions. This venting of one's feelings, as Brinker (1984) understood it, is not harmful to spectators; on the contrary, it serves their emotional balance of power (p. 21). It helps them maintain an equilibrium of mind and overcome their fear and hate. Catharsis is perceived as supporting one's emotional life and can help a person function better outside the theatre doors.

Using the concept of catharsis is not to demonstrate the theory of catharsis but to suggest that this concept can be useful for understanding the structure of social behavior in lounges, as well as the relationships and themes that evolve there.

We contend therefore that a process of catharsis is part of the social situation of teachers' lounges. The cathartic nature of these rooms is the answer to teachers' feelings of anger, frustration, fear, and pity, feelings that arise from the complex situations in which they are involved. Catharsis is a therapeutic need which helps to release emotions within the workplace. From our point of view, the high tension and conflicts that teachers face need to find a constructive channel of release. Catharsis relieves the social friction in teachers' lives; it is a profound process essential to teachers as a group. Since we are speaking about teachers as a community in the teachers' lounge, we define the catharsis there as a collective force by its very nature.

## Themes of Catharsis in Teachers' Lounges

Teachers are accustomed to "grumble" in the teachers' lounge, to loosen up, and to speak freely about everything that bothers them (Keinan 1994). In other words, they vent their frustrations. When colleagues encourage and support a teacher's outburst, the cathartic process takes on the characteristic of a social supportive function of healing, leading the teachers to sense an abatement of their negative feelings. If the outburst is rejected by his or her colleagues, the cathartic function is not fulfilled. In the teachers' room, teachers speak of their successes, their failures, and their professional fears. Their talk might extend beyond the current affairs of school life and include issues such as their low income, problems with the teachers' organization, or the failure of the municipality to supply basic school needs. However, the cathartic themes in the lounge usually concern the daily affairs of the school. The most common topics include: the insolence of a student, homework not being done, an undisciplined class, absenteeism of students, a dirty and messy classroom, and a general failure in exams. When a teacher enters the lounge he or she might relax and activate a collective cathartic process among the other teachers. This process usually develops as follows: A teacher enters the lounge, describes the problem, and talks about what is bothering him or her. The theme is usually familiar to other teachers who consequently react. Generally, owing to the fact that the problem must be dealt with immediately, the theme is taken up by a whole group of teachers. The topic is widely discussed; thus the cathartic process becomes collective.

## The Process of Collective Catharsis

The following cases illustrate the collective process of catharsis:

*Yardena's case*

> Yardena entered the teachers' lounge in a state of near hysteria. She shut the door behind her, leaned on it so that no one could come in, and then burst into tears: "If Talmon (the vice-principal who is in charge of organizing the time-table) continues to make announcements to my class without my consent, I will simply quit teaching." In response to Yardena's complaints, another teacher, Bath-Ami, told the group

> that a certain exam assigned for that day had been canceled without even consulting her. When she had entered the class with the prepared exams she was informed by her students that "Talmon had cancelled the exams." Sarah then remarked cynically that teachers who let themselves be treated like rubbish were stupid. There was an immediate reaction by all the other teachers in the lounge, many of whom had stories about the same theme. Collective catharsis reached its peak with raised voices, as teachers suggested ideas of resistance to the way the school was being managed. The collective involvement in the case served to relieve the anger and frustration.

Yardena's case can be viewed as an example of the healing aspect of catharsis due to the process of sharing multiple instances of the same phenomenon. The opportunity for sharing the frustrations and dissatisfactions in real time among colleagues might be perceived as leading to "purgation" of strong and negative feelings. Being part of collective catharsis enables all those present to participate in this process through re-living similar experiences.

Yardena's case is an example of the calming effect of collective catharsis which might not lead to in-depth rethinking of the school's practices. The dual aspects of the power of collective catharsis, either as a healing process, or as a destructive force, should be recognized as a component of school culture; both aspects need to be addressed.

*Shosh's case*

Shosh burst into the teachers' room crying out,

> I've had enough! From now on I won't try to look for alternative teaching methods. I will simply lecture all the time! The method of "chalk and talk" is all they [the students] deserve since they take advantage of the liberty I've given them. From now on they won't have any choice . . . " Shosh's emotional outburst triggered a response in Dana, a young teacher

> who had been struggling to find a solution to the same problem for a long time and had been blaming herself for not succeeding. Since Shosh is regarded as an experienced, skilled, and creative teacher, her outburst helped Dana, who was then able legitimately to tell of the difficulties she had experienced that morning. Dana had divided the class into working groups: one group went to work in the school grounds and had not returned to the class before the bell ending the lesson. Ruth said that the whole idea of dividing the class into working groups was useless, thereby arousing the rage of Ettie who was convinced that only poor teachers failed to deal with that method. A heated discussion on teaching methods enabled Dana to understand the complexity of the matter and overcome her feelings of frustration.

This case exemplifies an aspect of catharsis by which a certain truth is revealed through a process of "clarification." The discussion provided Dana with new insights into a complex matter concerning teaching.

Sometimes the incidents in lounges come close to rebellion. In such cases collective catharsis plays a crucial role as Hannah's case demonstrates:

*Hannah's case*

> One day in June, near the end of the school year, the junior high school students aged fourteen were to go on a field trip. As the time of departure came closer, the excitement and the anticipation grew among the students. However, due to difficult weather conditions, the school administration was forced to cancel the trip on the scheduled day. The forecast predicted a heat wave in the relevant area. Hannah had to confront her angry, frustrated students and functioned like a "sponge" absorbing their furious reaction and their disappointment. What made it especially difficult for her was the fact that she agreed with her students, and thought it was possible to go on the trip

despite the weather forecast. However, as a teacher, she could not express her opinion, or identify publicly with the students. The class rebelled, the students were asked to go home for their school bags, and then return to school for their regularly scheduled day. They refused. Hannah failed to persuade them; moreover, her anger with the school administration, which had placed her in such an awkward situation, grew. She became more irritable with her students whose remarks grew louder and more extreme regarding herself and the institution as a whole. She interpreted the "rebellion" as a sharp insult to her authority and, bursting into tears, she entered the teachers' lounge to try to calm down and find a solution. Inside the lounge, four other teachers, who taught the junior high classes, and who were supposed to escort them on the trip, had assembled. Except for one class all the students had responded in the same way. Hannah then grew aware of the new proportions of the problem which she had previously viewed as her personal problem only. The teachers exchanged views concerning the way in which the matter should be dealt with and finally they reached the conclusion that a different timetable for that day would serve as a sort of "mini" compensation for the students' disappointment. They decided to gather all the junior classes in the assembly hall and give details of their plan. However, the school principal refused to sanction this, fearing a general rebellion, and so forced the teachers to maintain the usual timetable. Dissatisfaction and discontent grew among the teachers. Meanwhile other teachers who had entered the teachers' lounge joined the arguments and, for some moments, it seemed as if there was no way out. The sense of solidarity prevented the problem from getting out of hand. After some time, the process of "collective catharsis" calmed the strong feelings. The teachers returned to their classes and each one treated the issue according to his or her inclination. Life in school returned to its usual course.

The topics of most importance to the majority of teachers in our study relate to discipline and coping with coverage of subject matter. Solutions, even if known to some extent theoretically, usually do not work. Practically, discipline problems will exist forever. There will always be too much material to be covered in too little time. These problems engender feelings of frustration and a sense of helplessness. Teachers do not feel they are masters of their professional fate. It must be noted that the process of collective catharsis which takes place in the teachers' lounge is practiced only for short periods of time. Due to the nature of the place and to the brief time teachers can stay there "between the ringings of the bell," the evolving context will always be one of being "between places," i.e., between a private place for teachers as opposed to a public place, the classroom. In the context of short time intervals, the cathartic process is bound to create a particularly sensitive situation.

*Esther's case*

Esther's case can be given as an example. Esther went through the cathartic process when she deliberately said:

> "I have never come across such stupid students before." This in turn created a chain of responses from the teachers present at that time in the lounge. The stress and emotional build-up were not relieved to any extent because the bell rang and interrupted the discussion. "In my opinion, it all begins in the teachers' lounge," says Dana, "however, it never comes to an end there."

A teacher's work at school deals mainly with emotions, and their lounge offers them support and serves as a shelter where one can laugh or cry without any interferance. As soon as their feelings are accepted as legitimate, they become members of the collective team, "one of the family."

Thus, tensions can be relieved in the teachers' room and enable the teacher to return to the class ready to teach.

## Concluding Comments

Dramatic concepts served to enrich our understanding of the interactions in lounges. Conventions were treated as complementary concepts shedding light on the social actions of teachers. The social function of catharsis in the lounge is perceived by us as necessary to the practice of teaching. We argue that through the process of collective catharsis teachers give meaning to their work by relieving the tensions and/or by looking for partners to share in the triumph and despair connected to their work experience.

Our cases strengthen the view of teachers not as solitary individuals, lonely in their classrooms, but as members of a vital community who share a common language. As will be demonstrated in the next chapter, analyzing events in dramatic terms allows us to refrain from psychological explanations, while still providing insights into teachers' actions in times of anger, stress, and tension or, conversely, in moments of joy and satisfaction.

# CHAPTER 4

# Blurring of Boundaries

In the previous chapters we looked at teachers' lounges from the point of view of social situations and dramatic concepts; now we turn to the elaboration of the dual function of these rooms as places for rest and work, continuing to use dramatic terms in our analysis of social situations. The notions of frontstage and backstage, as well as the distinction between private and public time, proxemics, and the physical dimensions of lounges guide our treatment of these issues. The questions we raised concern the blurring of boundaries with regard to lounges: What is the major function of these rooms in the lives of teachers in schools? Which features of the lounge make it possible to combine, for instance, functions of rest and work? What is the meaning of time spent in lounges?

## "Make-work"

Entering a teachers' lounge one immediately meets a businesslike atmosphere. At first glance it is difficult to describe what is going on and, if one tries to ask the teachers about the prevailing conventions of behavior in their lounge, they usually do not know what to answer. Teachers tend to take many of their conventions for granted, and they might not realize they have done so until an unusual incident occurs. For example, teachers were unaware of the fact that they sometimes tend to speak loudly and interrupt each other. We interfered in their usual 'businesslike' behavior by entering their lounge with our video camera. This unusual event made them question their behavior, their norms, and their world. While watching the video replay, they were astonished to find themselves asking each other to be quiet. The video offered them a surprising glance at the mirror, reflecting their life in the lounge.

Gross (1949), who studied social establishments, showed that different business offices have different norms concerning informal chatter among clerks. However, he indicates that only when we happen to study an office that has a sizable number of foreign immigrant employees, do we suddenly appreciate the fact that permission to engage in informal talk may not constitute permission to engage in informal talk in a foreign language. Goffman (1959) who refers to Gross, elaborates this idea and clarifies a form of conventions that has been studied in social establishments, namely, "make-work." He explains that it is understood in many establishments that not only will workers be required to produce a certain amount of work within a given period of time, but also that they will be ready, when called upon, to give the impression that they are working hard at that moment.

## Place

Are the notions of "make-work" or "make-no-work" integral parts of lives in lounges? Do teachers in their lounge need to use the "make-work" form of behavior? If so, before whom do they need to pretend they are working? Before their colleagues? Their students who might peep in? Or, possibly, their superiors? Beyond relating activities to the presence of other people, we raise a question about the relation of activities to a definition of place.

Woods (1984) considers the staffroom as the teachers' own area:

> The staffroom is the teachers' collective private area. (p. 191)

What is the nature of this "collective private area"? Is it a work or a rest area? What is the nature of work being done there? What are the characteristics of the lounge as a rest area?

We turn to some teachers' own perceptions of these functions. The perceived dichotomy between a work place and a rest area arises out of long conversations that we conducted with many teachers:

Jane, an English teacher, with eighteen years experience, said:

> There is a great paradox in this matter of lounges. On one hand, it is a place to relax in, away from work; we enter the lounge to "clean our heads," but if we listen to what we are talking about there, we can clearly see that only a few of us are not talking about work. It is rare that the subject is about anything but work. In fact we continue working even during our free periods, and despite this we love being there. I don't know how to explain it. However, I feel that I get a rest, even though I am working.

The lounge was defined in teachers' talk in terms of a place of work as well as a place to rest. Both terms define the room as an area which excludes the students. The exclusion of students is a common feature of staffrooms. Woods (1984) for instance states that:

> Pupils are often debarred from knocking on the door, or even approaching its vicinity, by "out-of-bounds" corridors. (p. 191)

Teachers maintained that whether it is considered a work place or a rest area, it is still a territory which belongs to them. This understanding is congruent with Goffman's (1959) perception concerning specific regions and behavior in regions. He elaborates the idea of a back region, of backstage:

> Backstage may be defined as a place, relative to a given performance, where the impression fostered by

> the performance is knowingly contradicted as a matter of course. There are, of course, many characteristic functions of such places. It is here that the capacity of a performance to express something beyond itself may be painstakingly fabricated; it is here that illusion and impressions are openly constructed . . . Here the performer can relax; he can drop his front, forgo speaking his lines, and step out of character. (p. 112)

This backstage activity is identified by Goffman as part of the teachers' lounge activities. Goffman added that:

> When pupils leave the school room and go outside for a recess of familiarity and misconduct, they often fail to appreciate that their teachers have retired to a "common room" to swear and smoke in a similar recess of backstage behavior. (p. 132)

The equating of the teachers' lounge with a backstage region is significant because it sets the room apart as an independent territory. It is an area which is separated from other parts of school. It is apart from classrooms, corridors, and offices and its identity is emphasized by its being enclosed within four walls.

Let us open one of these walls, the "fourth wall" for a moment and peep in to see and learn what's going on within. What kind of performances are conducted there, and for what purposes? According to Goffman, although the lounge constitutes a backstage region, we conceive of it as multidimensional; some of the activities there are a kind of "frontstage performance" because of the "blurring of boundaries" occurring in that area. The following episodes reflect this phenomenon:

Aware of the "fourth wall" convention we carefully watched performances in the lounge. We observed Johnny, a math teacher, forty years old, with over fifteen years of experience, for a few days:

Johnny used to stand, ready to close the teachers' lounge door, every single time that someone entered and left it open. He did it in a deliberate and systematic way, Johnny needed the clear division between inside and outside the lounge. It was essential for him that the teachers' area remain an exclusive territory: the students should not come in, and strangers should not intrude. He wanted all the indoor activities to be segregated. When any teacher stood in the doorway, talking to someone, one could observe how Johnny put himself into a "standby" condition. Once, while Esther, a literature teacher, had a long conversation with another teacher in the entrance, Johnny was unable to concentrate on anything. He could not take his eyes off the entrance. Our empathy toward him increased. We had a strong desire to tell him: "Look, why don't you go and ask them to close the door, instead of being disturbed in a way that paralyzes you?"

But our desire was restrained by the convention of the "forth wall." Johnny became edgy and angry. He began to mumble some meaningless words, and slowly involved those who sat near him in his problem, trying to convince them that it was of common interest. He burst out with: "This is "Hutzpa," this is a disgrace. Those people are talking endless nonsense in the doorway, as if no one else exists around here.

Other teachers who were sitting there appeared indifferent to what was going on. Some, even if they were annoyed, did not respond empathetically. At a certain moment, Johnny could bear it no longer. He stormed up to Esther, and shouted at her: "Move off, we want to close the door!"

Esther did not mind, and gave us no indication that Johnny's problem affected her. Maybe she was not even aware of his great distress. She said automatically: "Oh, yes, yes, of course," as a routine answer, but continued talking. Only the ringing of the bell

> saved the situation from deteriorating any further. Johnny quickly collected his belongings and ran out of the lounge to the classroom.

Unknown to him our empathy escorted him. We were worried since we knew he might carry with him the impact of the unrest he had experienced in the lounge.

## Backstage and Frontstage

How might one interpret the performance we had watched? Certainly it was not a rest period for Johnny; nor was it a work situation. In order to understand the situation, we used Goffman's (1959) observation that backstage behavior tends to be accompanied by informal language. He clarifies that

> The backstage language consists of reciprocal first-naming, co-operative decision-making, rough informal dress, "sloppy" sitting and standing posture, use of dialect or sub-standard speech, mumbling and shouting, playful aggressivity and "kidding," inconsiderateness for the other minor but potentially symbolic acts, minor physical self-involvements such as humming, whistling, chewing, nibbling, belching, and flatulence. The frontstage behavior language can be taken as the absence (and in some sense the opposite) of this. In general, the backstage conduct is one which allows minor acts which might easily be taken as symbolic of intimacy and disrespect for others present and for the region, while front region conduct is one which disallows such potentially offensive behavior. (p. 128)

Goffman's framework sheds new light on the situation. It helped us understand that backstage behavior can be characterized by activities such as Johnny's or Esther's, or anyone else who felt free to behave with "minor disrespect" toward those present. But for Johnny those activities could not be considered minor; rather they were perceived as essential. The paradox lies within the definition of the lounge area as a "public/private" one. Johnny wanted some privacy in terms of closed doors, in terms of complete segregation from the students and anyone else other than his colleagues. He understood the public element of the lounge to be manifested by teachers staying together in the same territory. Esther, on the other hand, understood privacy in less restricted terms. Here we come to the essence of the paradox, the essence of the duality in the functions of teachers' lounges. It is work versus rest; public versus private territory. A place for teachers to be alone and for a team to gather, a place of blurred boundaries. It might be argued that the room as a backstage region has its own characteristics but, above all, it is a place of blurred boundaries, and this is an unmistakable feature which characterizes the teachers' territory in schools.

We will describe another case; it took place during the lunch break:

> Ann, a chemistry teacher, burst into the teachers' lounge, threw her belongings down on the first table, slammed the door aggressively, then with her back pressing against it so that nobody could enter, stuttered: "I am fed up . . . I am fed up . . . " The few teachers who were there tried to comfort her: "Calm down," "Would you like a drink of water?" "Look, it's almost the end of the day, you're going home soon." Some teachers tried to find out what was wrong. Ann would not cool down. All the attempts to pacify her only increased her anger. It seemed as if she was wrestling with humiliation, some insult we did not know about, which she had brought with her from her class. She seemed weak and helpless.

Ann had crossed the boundary line. She had run away from the territory of the class to that of the lounge. The teachers' lounge was a safe haven for her, a refuge, where she could burst into tears. It was difficult to understand the details, but it was clear that she could not discipline her class. The students paid no attention to her instructions. Ann's behavior was unusual: it was an expression of her definition of the teachers' lounge as a private place. The distinction between a public and private area is made clearer. If teachers choose, they can close the door, draw the curtains, and relax from their role as teachers. The teacher can stop playing an authoritative figure and can be at ease, but only on condition that the atmosphere is supportive. The support of one's colleagues constitutes the collective aspect of the lounge. We have to bear in mind, though, that while a teacher like Ann might benefit from the support of her colleagues and their empathy, the situation could have been reversed if the lounge had, at that moment, exhibited its public face.

The blurring of boundaries, mentioned above, might create in-between situations, such as exemplified by Johnny's experiences in the lounge. While Johnny seemed to be completely immersed in his perception of the "backstage" character of the lounge, other teachers were apparently more inclined to view the lounge as a "frontstage" domain.

The backstage region of teachers' life in school can be seen as a place for different kinds of behavior and conduct. It is also a site for feeling emotionally secure within a community consisting of one's colleagues. Beyond this haven of intimacy and support, the lounge might also be viewed as providing the psychological space to allow teachers the freedom and protection for learning from each other and from one's own experiences, whether successful or not. According to Schwab (1978), young learners need a "psychological space" to engage in trial efforts and,

> to be assured that attempts at doing and thinking will be accepted as attempts, as trial runs and practices, and not as definitive measures of his own powers or limitations. (p. 114)

We see teachers as sharing this need, which is justified to a certain extent by the support of colleagues in the lounge.

But the teachers do not always find the relaxation they are looking for. Some lounges are threatening and unpleasant, and not a place of refuge. Such rooms may possess the physical aspects of lounges, but not the emotional ones. When a room lose its sense of support and the meaning of haven, it ceases to be backstage, and becomes frontstage, where teachers need to wear a mask and hide any sign of weakness in order to cope with their colleagues. They must pretend that they are part of a team, but they know that they are on their own.

Observing teachers' behavior in the lounge, one can sense if they feel they are "backstage" or in a front region. The structure in a given teachers' lounge will be seemingly the same but, if teachers feel it is a frontstage region, manners will be formal and polite and the element which Goffman called "appearance" will obviously dominate the scene. Backstage can become frontstage under some circumstances. These often depend upon the way the teachers perceive the job and climate of the workplace. Thus an important aspect of teachers' lounges is the fact that the area may be neither backstage nor frontstage, but can be both at the same time for different people. For some, it might be considered as backstage while for others it is frontstage. Moreover, we observed that sometimes the essence of the same area could change for the same person depending on the time, the context, and the mood of the teacher.

A painful example of this sudden transformation was seen in an incident with Sarah:

> Sarah brought a cake to the teachers' lounge about a week after the summer vacation. She set the cake out on one of the tables and invited everyone in the room to take a piece, to celebrate the wedding of her daughter who was a graduate of the school. Sarah was so relaxed she could admit that she was "fed up" with working. "I'm ready to retire, and help bring up my own grandchildren." Ron, a school executive responded: "The students will be happy to agree with you." The peaceful atmosphere immediately turned

> upside down. Sarah controlled her anger and hurt, but could no longer continue with her relaxed backstage performance. She became tense. Her friend Ruth tried to save the situation by loudly joking: "Of course the students would be happy if we all retired." Teachers began to laugh. They continued eating and talking as before but it was clear that, for Sarah, the intimacy of the teachers' lounge was lost, as was the sense of belonging.

For Sarah, who had started out with a sense of being "backstage" and was relaxed enough to voice her feelings about work, there came a rude awakening. Suddenly, she was in a "frontstage" situation. This blurring of boundaries can be very demanding. The amount of energy needed to perform backstage, not knowing when it may turn into frontstage, is enormous. The tensions involved in such performances can explain part of the constant energized state in which teachers work and live. On the one hand, there are defined territories in school but, on the other, life within the teachers' world is multifaceted, because of the constant blurring of boundaries. The socio-temporal aspects of lounges constitute another area of blurring of boundaries.

### Time

According to Lieberman & Miller in *Teachers, Their World, and Their Work* (1984)

> All teachers need a place to relax, a time to hide from students.

They also mention the idea that

> a unique faculty culture is forged during the time teachers spend together as part of the routine of the school day. (p. 47)

We mention this in order to understand the nature of the time that teachers spend together in their "public/private" domain. Hargreaves, Hestor & Mellor (1984) identify and analyze five principal phases concerning time that are common to virtually all lessons:

1. The "entry" phase
2. The "settling down" or preparation phase
3. The "lesson proper" phase
4. The "clearing up" phase
5. The "exit" phase

The authors claim pupils know which rules are to be enforced according to which phase they are in; and the same goes for the teacher. When speaking of lounges, we have to consider the rules of another game. By analyzing teachers' lounges using the framework of time, we can define four phases that enable us to understand the rules of the teachers' lounge. The four principal phases common to all teachers' lounges are:

1. The "entry" phase
2. The "exit" phase
3. The "free time" phase
4. The "between the rings of the bell" phase

It is important to note that in Israeli schools these phases are not necessarily synchronized for all the staff. Some teachers arrive and depart early, and some later in the day.

## The "Entry" Phase

This is the time spent before the beginning of the day's work. Some teachers prefer to enter the classroom immediately upon arriving at school; most of them, however, choose to start their day by first visiting the teachers' lounge, which serves as their backstage. This phase prior to all activities of the school day constitutes a situation of fortifying oneself by means of refreshment such as drinking the morning cup of coffee or tea. This daily regular phase of "entry" is characterized by the "good morning" greetings exchanged among colleagues along with such general questions as "How are you today?", "How long are you staying today?", "Do you expect anything special today?" etc. The social actions practiced during that period are of a routine nature, such as hanging up one's coat, preparing coffee or tea, lighting a cigarette, and other acts that foster a feeling of relaxation before engaging in the daily confrontations taking place on the frontstage. However, this clear, calm, and simple state of "entry" alters during the day. The "entry" phase for teachers who start their work at ten o'clock and not at eight o'clock, for instance, might have totally different characteristics, since their colleagues are engaged at that time in another phase, such as the "between the rings of the bell" phase or the "exit" phase. This disparity represents a blurring of boundaries between phases, and might cause misunderstandings and uncomfortable situations. We mentioned in chapter 2, which deals with social situations, that there are certain norms of time-use in the lounge. The ringing of the bell is a sign for teachers to return to their classrooms. When some teachers are in the exit phase, and in no hurry to leave the lounge, their colleagues may be in the "between the bells" phase and have to return to their classrooms; this might lead to some confusion about each other's intentions and behaviors. For instance, two teachers who work together on a common project, or who are personal friends, might find themselves in an embarrassing situation when one has to hurry and break off a conversation because she is "between the bells" while her colleague is on the point of entry or exit. One is already on "private time" while the other is still very much engaged in the duties of "public time."

### The "Exit" Phase

This refers to the time interval before returning home, a period that concludes the day's work. For some teachers, this is a brief phase in which they reenact almost the same activities they performed during their "entry" phase. Again they greet their fellow colleagues, this time to say farewell and make comments, such as "Have a nice day," "See you tomorrow," "How was your day?" Following these remarks, they usually take their belongings and depart. But there are teachers for whom the "exit" phase is an opportunity to relax; for them it is a period of time which offers them some rest without any obligations whatsoever. It is "private time." Thus some teachers intentionally choose to extend their stay in the teachers' lounge in order to engage in conversation with their colleagues. "Exit" time is usually connected with gossiping and exchanging stories. It is the period during which teachers feel a sense of belonging to a group, yet have no immediate obligations to that group. They are free to leave whenever it is comfortable or necessary to do so. It is interesting that even those teachers who have small children to take care of, and need to rush back home to their domestic duties, confess that they would like to stay in the teachers' lounge because of the events taking place there, such as sharing stories and information, arranging the work load and, in general, enjoying a period of transition between the workplace and home.

## The "Free Time" Phase

Metaphorically speaking, teachers refer to this time period in terms of "the free period" or, in Israel, "a window." On the one hand, teachers are free to engage in their private affairs but, on the other, they might also wish to take advantage of every spare moment for their work. There are schools in which it is compulsory for teachers to remain in the lounge during their free period, so that they may be able to substitute for an absent teacher. For this reason one might come across teachers sitting in the staffroom, partly hidden, for fear of being called to substitute for a missing colleague. However, one can characterize this period as a period free from teaching which is often used to prepare for class. Woods (1984) describes such periods:

> On these occasions the staffroom is used as a "quiet area" in the service of the official work of the institution. (p. 191)

### The "between the Rings of the Bell" Phase

Such periods of time provide the most frequent and regular time spent in the teachers' lounge. In its very essence, this 'intermediate period' is well known for its tension and sense of urgency due to the fact that moving from one class to another, as Israeli teachers do, is particularly demanding. At this time the teacher tries to converse with other teachers over specific matters that need to be dealt with immediately, as well as catch a brief moment with the class homeroom teacher about, let us say, a trip that is due to take place the following day. This is clearly a case of "public time." Moreover, in addition to these tasks, it is often necessary to return or pick up a book from the library, and to read the new instructions and information on the notice board. In contrast to the many activities the teachers must cope with, this period is very short and lasts only five or ten minutes at the most, excluding one period of break, longer than the others, which lasts up to twenty minutes. Metaphor expressions such as "beehive," "hen house," or "a railway station" are often used by teachers to refer to such periods and these are extremely appropriate expressions. This period is considered a difficult time for the teacher, who is literally being asked to achieve the impossible, that is, to rest and work at the same time, to relax, and yet to fulfill many other duties with full energy and strength, all of which results in the inevitable conclusion that this race against the clock is sure to fail from the very start.

The four principal time phases that have been suggested as common to all teachers' lounges acquire their own norms and conventions, resulting from the nature of the lounge and its functions. These phases form the rhythm of the lounges, its recurring and alternating temporal structures which shape the experiences of teachers in the lounge.

The question arises whether the time occupied in the teachers' lounge should be considered a time for relaxation, as "private time," or a time dedicated to work, and thus defined as "public time." This dilemma may sometimes be solved by teachers themselves by changing their perception of the situation; as one teacher, stated, "I don't know how to explain it: I feel that I'm resting even though I am working."

There is no doubt that this situation is a result of ambiguous components. The teachers' lounge supplies coffee and comfortable chairs to rest on yet, at the same time, information is being exchanged verbally, or through reading of the notice board. During recesses teachers meet their colleagues; and matters of work, problems of students, and countless other issues must be dealt with before the recess ends. The teacher is thus caught in a web, embedded in the blurred boundaries of "private" versus "public time."

At the beginning of this chapter we asked whether "make-work" or "make-no-work" are integral parts of teachers' lives in lounges. As our discussion of the "blurring of boundaries" in the lounge has shown, both "work" and "no-work" find their place according to the phase in which teachers find themselves.

A comprehensive discussion of the distinction between public and private time is to be found in the work of Eviatar Zerubavel (1981). In his *Hidden Rhythms* he argues that

> Time seems to function as a segmenting principle. Similar to the way in which it helps to keep the sacred domain and the profane domain apart, it also helps to segregate the private and the public spheres of life from one another, as well as to separate persons from each in their various social roles. (p. 14)

Zerubavel claims that time is evidently the most significant dimension of the "total" aspect of "total institutions" in general. He suggests

> that we view the relative degree of the individual's social accessibility at any given time as a proportion

> between two hypothetical constructs, "private time" and "public time." "Private time" is essentially "sociofugal" in the sense that like certain socially defined spaces, it is deliberately designed to prevent, or at least discourage, the formation of human contact and to separate people from one another. Public time on the other hand, is essentially "sociopetal," in the sense that like various other spaces, it is deliberately meant to promote the establishment of human contact and to draw people together. (p. 143)

Zerubavel warns us that privacy or inaccessibility must not be regarded as absolute notions, since they are essentially defined as having a relative relation:

> Private or public quality of any given space very often varies across time. Private 'back regions' for example wherein individual are isolated from being observable by their audience are defined not only in spatial terms but in temporal terms as well. (p. 140)

This notion is also presented by Goffman (1959):

> There are many regions which function at one time and in one sense as a front region and at another time and in another sense as a back region. (p. 126)

Thus, the blurring of boundaries in lounges might be understood as pertaining to the territorial aspects of the lounge, which are both "private" and "public," "frontstage" as well as "backstage," and the temporal aspects of the lounge, which reflect both "private" and "public" time. The actual physical space of the lounges plays an important role in determining the social interactions and might give rise to the blurring of boundaries.

## Proxemics

Proxemics is a term that was first coined by Hall (1959), an anthropologist in the fifties, who investigated the idea of one's personal space in order to develop his theory of reciprocal reactions among people in a defined space. In his research he defines four different spaces: intimate space, personal space, social space, and public space. The intimate space refers to friendship, closeness, and love. This is the distance between eight and eighteen inches whereby a person is always conscious of his/her partner. The personal space in which the distance is eighteen to forty-eight inches is meant for private conversations. This distance is the ordinary distance when two people meet by chance in the street. The social and the public spaces are both at a distance of four to seven feet and there is almost no difference between them in this respect. Rather, the difference is in the nature of the activity that takes place. Both are spaces without privacy.

Teachers' lounges dictate conditions of intimate and personal spaces due to the high density of "inhabitants" in a relatively small place. One can find a certain paradox in the very fact that the lounge can be defined as a public place without privacy whereas, according to the proxemics approach, life in the lounge exists in personal and intimate spaces. The notion of proxemics entails the examination of the physical relations of closeness versus distance among people in a given place or time. These relations project certain attitudes of people toward each other in the situation in which they find themselves. In other words, the concept of proxemics reflects a person's condition in a given space and time and enables us to read the nonverbal signs of communication that take place, such as gestures, facial expressions, glances, and movements. Very often one finds a mismatch between verbal and nonverbal communication and one usually tends to believe more the nonverbal forms of expression.

In the previous chapter we dealt with dramatic expressions in the lounge. The theatrical framework aids us to better understand the nature of proxemics in these rooms. In the theatre, the concept of proxemics is central. It reflects dynamic relationships between the characters on stage, and only through their positioning on stage can one read these relationships. Since the theatre operates on borrowed space and time, it separates itself from everyday life. Hence, proxemics in a theatre becomes the process of raising the audience's awareness of the relationships among the characters in the play, their functioning in multifaceted space and scenery.

Activity in the lounge resembles activity in the theatre. It takes place in a closed arena and is constrained by limits of time and participants. We suggest the possibility of looking at the multifaceted scenery of teachers' lounges from a proxemics perspective as a way of "decoding" and making sense of the inherent power relationships among teachers in the lounge. A teacher entering the lounge might be able to decipher the power and/or friendship relationships at first glance by becoming aware of the positions people occupy in the space. Such a glance is similar to a spectator's view through the fourth wall who perceives the scenario all at once. Hannah's story as a novice teacher is a clear example of how the physical positioning of a person within the confines of a lounge delineates her social situation. Standing for a long time on one spot near the coffee machine, far from the closely knit group of her colleagues, Hannah tells the observer that for this moment at least she does not belong. Not only do we, as observers, sense the situation in this way, but the participants themselves use the space to express their feelings of intimacy or detachment.

We have discussed place, time, and proxemics as providing us with some insights into the incidents in lounges. These take place in the physical reality of lounges, to which we turn now.

## The Physical Reality in Different Teachers' Lounges: The Teachers' View

What are some of the principles of school buildings that shape the physical reality of lounges? Let us listen to the voices of teachers describing their lounges.

One teacher, with twenty-three years of experience in the same large elementary school of five hundred students, situated in a small town, describes her lounge as follows:

> The lounge is in a separate building which houses the offices of the principal, the school secretary, several laboratories, and a special education class. The other classes occupy three additional buildings. The entrance to our building is out of bounds for students so that the teachers can enjoy some quiet during breaks. The lounge is noisy enough as it is. The lounge had been originally planned as a classroom. Inside there is a mirror, a present from the teachers' union, possibly for teachers to make themselves presentable before entering their classes. On the wall you can always find numerous announcements concerning school activities. On a table there is additional material for teachers, such as special staff development stuff. A small refrigerator stands near this table. A case with lockers made by older students serves as storage place for the teachers. On an ugly table stands a water heater and above it hangs a small cupboard. I have banged my head against this cupboard thousands of times. It holds coffee, tea and sugar which is usually full of ants. In the corner there is a sink and above it a place for cups and saucers. Two large windows provide enough light. This year the graduating class bought curtains for the windows. We usually sit at our regular places around a large square table, facing each other. The table is very stable and also serves as a work area. Some of the chairs are comfortable and some are old and extremely uncomfortable. A white plastic tablecloth covers the table. I personally liked it more before when we had linen and flower pots, it was more homelike then. Still, the atmosphere is fairly pleasant, it is hard to leave the lounge when the bell rings, and that is a sign that we like being there.

Another teacher, with fourteen years of experience in an elementary school, also with about five hundred students, situated in a middle-class suburban area describes her lounge thus:

> Our lounge is in the central school building, almost at the entrance, close to the janitor's room. The principal and the secretary are on a floor above the lounge. The room is too small and there is not enough room for teachers who would like to rest, or to conduct quiet conversations with colleagues. Three large tables were put together to form a square and the teachers sit around them. Two main groups have formed: the teachers with seniority, and those who are relatively new to the school; a lot of interaction takes place between the groups. We have a small kitchenette for preparing hot drinks. The walls are covered with announcements but we have also added pictures. We try hard to cultivate the aesthetic aspects of the lounge; we made nice curtains for the windows, and we often change the tablecloth. Coffee drinking is a highly valued ritual in which everyone participates, teachers, secretaries and janitor alike. Students are not allowed in the lounge, though sometimes students with problems will enter the lounge, but then a teacher will go outside with them. The children get the message that their teachers are tired after teaching and deserve a period of rest. Sometimes students will crowd around the lounge door, but whoever is close to the door will tell them not to disturb the teachers. Still, when I want quiet, I go to the yard, which is very beautiful, and sit on one of the benches there. I would like to feel in the lounge like at home, with the physical and interpersonal atmosphere close and warm, but I don't know if this can be achieved.

These teachers seem to view their lounges as an extension of home, emphasizing the warmth of friendship and interpersonal relationships between peers. They tend to celebrate their birthdays and to note family occasions in the lounge. One teacher commented:

> We pay special attention to the cultivation of a pleasant and friendly atmosphere in the lounge. Eight years ago there were twenty teachers in our school; now there are forty-five of us and we still feel close to each other—like in a family.

The expressed longing of these teachers for a homelike atmosphere in their lounges might be interpreted as reflecting a blurring of boundaries between the niches of home and work. This linking of home and school is perceived by us to be similar to the teacher's image of the "classroom as home" as analyzed by Clandinin (1986). Clandinin sees this image as highlighting

> the experiential link between a teacher's educational and personal private life. (p. 131)

The need to feel "at home" in the lounge, to use one of the teachers' expressions, may be understood as well to reflect the teacher's need for a place of relaxation, for a time-out from work. The following description is another portrait of a lounge, serving the double functions of a homelike place where one can rest as well as a place of work:

> Last week, I visited the teachers' lounge at the school of Arts in Tel-Aviv . . . he way to the teachers' lounge is located along a well-maintained corridor, its walls presenting hammered copper works that incorporate the subject "Jerusalem of gold and of copper . . ." There are paintings as well as realistic [icons of] pop culture, such as the display of a sneaker, or the yellow of an egg in a frying pan. There is also a huge cage with twittering parrots. At the entrance to the teachers' lounge two human-size dolls capture one's attention. They are displayed sitting at a table which is

> covered with a red tablecloth; [a] cream pie and two cups of coffee are evident. These dolls, on loan from the theatre collection, characterize the unique atmosphere of the school (which is for students of special artistic talent from all over the city) and, at the same time, they also create an aesthetic, theatrical, amusing atmosphere within the teachers' lounge.
>
> The high square tables, constructed according to the teachers' requirements so that they could also be used as working tables, are covered with red tablecloths and placed all over the room. The windows are covered with matching curtains, made by the mother of one of the students. A colored shelf is placed there, on which a random collection of empty bottles, and three flower pots are displayed. The kitchenette, including an old refrigerator, donated by parents, is part of the teachers' lounge and is constantly in use. At the end of the room there is the "living room"—an intimate sitting corner, which consists of an old sofa, two couches and a low coffee table, all contributed by parents. The colorful patchwork tablecloth and all the cushions were made by the students and the art teacher. This niche is commonly referred to as the "corner," where teachers can converse intimately. At times it serves as an alternative resting area for a sick student. Another interesting item I came across was the telephone which was placed over a straw "elephant" near a small chair which enables the teachers to receive their telephone calls in their room rather than in the secretaries' office. There is also a copying machine available for the staff. However, the teachers claim they hardly ever have time to simply sit and rest in their lounge.

Viewing teachers' lounges through the eyes of the teachers themselves highlights some of the commonalties experienced by those using different lounges. Interest in the relationship between the characteristics of physical environments and human conduct was first developed during the late 1960s. Thus, one comes across architects, town planners, interior designers, and landscape designers, who deal with an enormous range of subjects; these subjects can vary from the influences of the characteristics of a certain territory upon the behavior of its inhabitants, to the influences of the characteristics of any room, including its furnishings, upon the behavior of the people in it. Experts have set themselves the goal of understanding the relationship between behavior and human experience with regard to the physical environment (Wolfe & Proshansky 1974). The physical attributes of lounges described above create the setting for the blurring of boundaries between home and workplace, frontstage and backstage, and private and public time.

## Concluding Comments

The various descriptions of teachers' lounges presented in this chapter reflect the spatial and functional divisions between work and rest, public and private, in the lounge. The notion of proxemics illustrates how teachers might position themselves in the physical space of the lounge according to the nature of their interactions.

The blurring of boundaries is most apparent in the case of how teachers learn in the teachers' learning in the lounge through an exchange of experiences. This kind of learning benefits from the backstage and private features of the lounge yet is focused on professional issues. The cyclical and temporal structure of schooling and classrooms has been treated by Clandinin & Connelly (1986) and Connelly & Clandinin (1986). School cycles have temporal boundaries that are usually rigid and resemble, according to Zerubavel (1979), "glass walls in that they are usually taken for granted, thus becoming practically invisible, until someone tries to walk through them" (p. 2). Connelly & Clandinin (1990) claim that because the "glass wall" nature of boundaries is taken as normal in schools, efforts are sometimes made to overcome the rigidity. In our study of life in teachers' lounges we found temporal boundaries to be not rigid but permeable, allowing teachers to function professionally and socially in a limited space and time. In this chapter we have tried to illustrate how teachers act in lounges, weaving their way between opposite sides, trying to be as efficient as possible in the inherent situation of blurred boundaries.

The understanding of the blurring of boundaries in the lounge brings to our attention the constant emotional burden experienced by teachers. The language that teachers use when talking and writing about lounges reveals diverse situations of blurred boundaries and the frames of mind that accompany them.

# CHAPTER 5

# Metaphors and Monologues

What can be learned from teachers' metaphors and monologues about their experiences in lounges? Do teachers speak in one voice when talking about lounges? Are there any prominent features in their descriptions and expressions?

In the previous chapters we have tried to describe, analyze, and interpret life in teachers' lounges, applying social and dramatic frameworks. The culture of teachers' lounges as we have seen is intricate, layered, and in constant flux, though it also exhibits recurring features. In comparison with lounges, classrooms present a more straightforward picture. In classrooms we usually have one or two teachers and a specific number of students. The functions of the classroom are clearly delineated—teachers teach and students learn. Sarason (1996) argues that the regularities of schools are truly amazing. He states that

> Beginning in the first grade and continuing throughout the elementary and secondary school years, every child on every school day receives instruction and drill in the use of numbers. This is an amazing regularity within the school culture. I confess to not understanding why this is so. Why must first grade children be exposed to such instruction and drill? Why must arithmetic and mathematics be taught every year? For the child, teacher, and arithmetic supervisor (among others), arithmetic is a part of a

> highly structured day. I am tempted to say that it is an involuntary activity of each day but that would be quite wrong, because to everyone concerned that is the way it is and that is the way it should be. But are there no alternative ways of looking at arithmetic in terms of when or how often it should be taught? (p. 27)

Sarason discusses the power of these regularities and their impact on any attempt to introduce changes into schooling. In spite of the fluid nature of the culture of lounges, teachers' lounges also display several regularities in the interplay of the two main functions which characterize them, namely, according to our study, the social-rest and the work functions.

The four temporal phases in lounges: "entry," "exit," "free time," and "between the bells," are examples of regularities common to many teachers' lounges. A rich and colorful portrait of the regularities was disclosed through our analysis of the metaphors and monologues that teachers use to describe their lounges; some of these are presented in the following paragraphs.

## Metaphors

In the last two decades the use of metaphors has increased in the study of education, (Berliner 1990; Collins & Green 1990; Munby & Russell 1990). Black (1979) defines the metaphor as new metamorphosis of meaning by moving schemes between unrelated areas. The metaphor creates new meanings, and it is possible to compare its power to a stone thrown into a lake that results in a series of ever-growing circles.

The power of the metaphor lies in creating inspiring associations. Lakoff & Johnson (1980) see in the metaphor an instrument that shapes our way of thinking:

> Metaphor structures our thinking, our understanding of events and consequences our behavior . . . Metaphor is principally a way of conceiving of one

thing in terms of another and its primary function is of understanding. (p. 36)

We were interested in learning about teachers' metaphors in relation to their lounges. An open-ended component of the questionnaire, referred to in chapter 1, "Modes of Inquiry," provided teachers with an opportunity to suggest metaphors that described their lounges. Their responses were analyzed and added insights into the possible role that lounges play in the lives of teachers.

From the analysis of the teachers' answers, we elicited five root metaphors which dominate the teachers' way of speaking about their lounges. Such metaphors are:

1. The teachers' lounge as a beehive.
2. The teachers' lounge as home.
3. The teachers' lounge as a kitchen.
4. The teachers' lounge as a coffee shop.
5. The teachers' lounge as a central station.

Each "root metaphor" emerges out of a cluster of images centered around a similar concept (Turner 1976).

## Root Metaphor: The Teachers' Lounge as a Beehive

*Cluster of Images: Beehive, Chicken Coop, Market, Stormy Place*

The most prevalent metaphor of the teachers' lounge describes the room as a beehive, which connotes a place of intense activity where events are incessantly occurring. The obvious association is that of productive busy bees. This metaphor uses the concrete image of the beehive to describe the constant motion of the teachers' lounge. The metaphor also suggests a warning that, in that place, agitated and restless behavior could take place as well.

The metaphor of the teachers' lounge as a chicken coop expresses the concept of business very clearly. In this image, a mocking sexist element is indicated. The "chicken coop" can be associated with futile talk and hollow chattering. The "market" metaphor introduces the meaning of selling and buying—thus the dimension of busy activity receives an alternative flavor: that of no-nonsense business.

A beehive, a chicken coop, and a market all contain within them the elements of disquiet and crowdedness. These images encompass aggression and turbulence. The primary characteristics of teachers in a room that functions as a beehive is business; "public time" dominates their "private time." The "beehive" metaphor is closely related to the work function of the lounge. Essentially, the teachers do live in incessant noise and, in this context, it is not difficult to understand their longing for a quiet place that would serve as home, as implied by the next root metaphor.

## Root Metaphor: The Teachers' Lounge as Home

*Cluster of Images: Home, Living Room, Dining Room, Family Room, Shelter*

The teachers' lounge as "home" and the other images in this cluster are in direct opposition to the beehive, chicken coop, and market metaphors. The intimacy, closeness, and the need for real contacts are indicated in the use of this metaphor. The main advantage of the "home" metaphor lies in its relation to the lounge in terms of a supportive, protective atmosphere. Its main disadvantage is that it offers an illusion of safety in a place that is ruled by transitions and essential uncertainty concerning one's place in the teachers' community. School is not home, and the lounge might offer its inhabitants a sense of shelter which cannot be substantiated.

The metaphor of the teachers' lounge as home strengthens the positive interpretation of this place and builds on the concept of "family." The term "family" in its positive sense, reflects mutual commitment, loyalty, and certain shared norms of behavior. From this point of view, one might derive features of professional collegiality, and characteristics of a "good colleague," as someone to be trusted, whose loyalty is taken for granted. Certain images are suggested in this context: The teachers' lounge as a "living room" or "dining room" are expressions of the functions that the lounge fulfills in the lives of some of the teachers. The "living room" is an expression of a need for a place where a pleasant, comfortable atmosphere can be developed. The "home" metaphor is closely related to the perceived social function of teachers' lounges.

### Root Metaphor: The Teachers' Lounge as a Kitchen

*Cluster of Images: Kitchen, Study Room, Operation Room, Conference Room*

This metaphor is close to the "home" metaphor in the sense that it expresses feelings of warmth, belonging, and confidence. On the other hand, this metaphor encompasses the notion of a "process"—the idea of "cooking." The kitchen metaphor relates to the teachers' lounge as a central place in which really important activities take place. The meaning of "cooking" is close to basic needs, of being engaged in important work.

The terms "operation room," "conference room," and "study" express a place where a conjunction of activities, emotions, ideas, struggles, and decisions are being made. Everyday feelings and routine activities are expressed in images that define the teachers' lounge in its professional, working aspect.

### Root Metaphor: The Teachers' Lounge as a Coffee Shop

*Cluster of Images: Coffee Shop, Cafeteria, Lobby*

These figures of speech suggest that the teachers' lounge is a place of rest and entertainment, a place where the atmosphere is easygoing, a place where one can take off one's professional uniform and take a break. Though both the metaphor of "home" and of "coffee shop" reflect rest and pleasure, one way of differentiating between them is through the degree of openness that they represent. While "home" and its dining room are private areas which are closed to strangers unless specifically invited there, the "coffee shop" metaphor expresses openness; anyone may enter a coffee shop or a cafeteria. These different metaphors can be perceived as accounting for teachers' behavior in the lounge. For instance, the teacher who guards the door of his lounge and tries to keep it closed so that strangers will not be able to enter might be understood to be acting out the "home" metaphor. The image of a "coffee shop" suits the organic structure of the school, as a system that functions between the bells, a place where all territories are "open to view," except for the teachers' lounge that periodically functions as "back stage." Here social relations can be developed and strengthened before the next task is to be undertaken. In a cafeteria, time is private—one can choose one's partners, and one can choose with whom to speak.

### Root Metaphor: The Teachers' Lounge as a Central Station

*Cluster of Images: Central Station, Bus Stop, Railway Station, Transit Point, Gas Station*

This metaphor reflects the transitional dimension of the teachers' lounge. Finding oneself in a station means staying there for a short period only, since the place itself has no importance of its own; its role lies in its being on the way to other destinations. From this point of view, the metaphor of a central station is in contrast to the metaphors of kitchen or home which contain within them the elements of warmth and stability.

The idea of a "transit point" emphasizes the elements of motion and noise: a place of casual, superficial meetings. The lounge as a "railway station" adds flavor to this notion and emphasizes the element of noise.

Calling the teachers' lounge a "transit point" diminishes its importance and links it with territories of minor importance. In contrast to this there is another image, that of a "gas station." Although this image also conveys a sense of the transitory nature of the lounge, it has an additional meaning. Basically, this image could be associated with the "kitchen metaphor" or even with the "home metaphor." Here, the room is seen as a place where, even if one stays there only for a short period of time, it is, as the teachers put it, "like a breath of oxygen," or "like air for breathing." The lounge functions as a place where one can metaphorically "recharge one's batteries," i.e., replenish one's resources.

All five root metaphors characterize how teachers view their lounges as a complex of contradictory entities. Each metaphor encompasses reality, as they see it. Addressing the nature of the lounges via the root metaphors, allowed us to gain insights into teaching and into the teachers' lives from the perspective of their sanctuary: their own "backstage" domain. The social situation in lounges is complex. Conceptualizing the reality of the staffroom through five "root metaphors" provides us with an imaginative, yet quite graphic, view of the culture of lounges, as seen by the teachers themselves.

By listening to their voices describing their lounges metaphorically, we were attuned to their emotional involvement with the lounge.

## Monologues about the Lounge: Teachers' Voices

Over the last ten years there has been a growing emphasis on addressing the voice of the teacher as a primary source for understanding the reality of classrooms and of teachers' professional lives.

We invite the reader now to listen to the voices of teachers as they present themselves in monologues entitled "My Life in the Teachers' Lounge." Through these monologues, it is possible to relate to the social and professional complexity of situations in the lounge as they see them, to become aware of their feelings of belonging in contrast to their feelings of alienation, and to gain insights into the way in which a community of discourse develops among members of a teaching staff.

We assumed that through the monologues each teacher would be able to express his or her authentic feelings without the intervention of a researcher. A monologue is an autonomous unit of discourse. It is a complete set of statements that can be used in order to understand the meanings assigned by the writer to the object in question, in this case, "My Life in the Teachers' Lounge." The monologues were obtained in response to a "call for monologues" on this topic. The response was extensive and included primary and junior high school teachers, student teachers, and people from various positions in the educational system.

We wanted to listen to the voices of teachers expressing their own, personal opinions. The experiences of teachers differ from person to person. The language and quality of the descriptions are different, but we can find an authentic expression of teachers' experiences and concerns in all of them. Although each monologue is the expression of one voice, we were able to discern the trend of a collective voice that emerged from all the monologues.

These written monologues contribute to an awareness of the teachers' own feelings toward the lounges. They were able to release pent-up feelings, and to put their thoughts in perspective as seen by the following comment: "Until I wrote this monologue I did not realize how much the lounge affected me."

## The Love-hate Attitude toward Lounges

We chose to illustrate the range of different voices through a continuum of attitudes toward the lounge. At one end we find Milla's voice:

> I hate to go to school because I hate to go into the lounge.

Milla teaches in a primary school and this is her fourth year there. At the other end, we hear Leah's voice:

> Sometimes in the middle of the lesson I find myself looking forward to the bell that will rescue me from the seriousness and the tension of the lesson. I like the atmosphere in the lounge and I want to be there.

Between these two poles of love-hate, there are feelings of closeness, love and belonging to a social-professional community, as well as feelings of alienation, anger, and harsh criticism. Within this range we can find various attitudes. Lina writes:

> It's a nice place, my lounge, and you don't feel how time passes, because I feel very comfortable with my friends.

Ruth writes:

> sit in the lounge but I still don't feel that I belong there though I feel close to the teachers.

Eva:

> I spend a lot of time in the lounge outside of working hours just to talk, share ideas, to work, to plan, or just to chat.

Leslie:

> I met a new first-year teacher who complained that she didn't belong in the lounge. This made her think that she would like to move to another school.

In order to uncover the voices within the written monologues, we chose three dimensions for analysis: one pertains to the value that the teacher attributes to the role of the lounge; a second dimension relates to the explicit and implied messages concerning lounges; and the third perspective is the interplay between accounts of incidents in the lounge and the attitudes toward these incidents. We will use these three dimensions as we analyze the following monologues.

The following is a short monologue of a new teacher, one in her third year of teaching; it focuses on the issue of why Sue prefers to distance herself from the lounge:

Sue:

> I worked as a teacher last year. The worst part wasn't coping with teaching or with the children, but the time spent during the break. I would have preferred to stay in the yard and talk to the children rather than sit in the lounge. Sometimes during the winter I would prefer staying in the classroom to entering the lounge. The difficult part was to sit with them [the teachers] and to find a starting point from which I could join the bunch of veteran teachers, some of whom had taught me in the past. Sometimes I would take with me material [to the lounge] to prepare for the kids or just reading material, and sometimes I would think about things that were detached from what the teachers were talking about. Here was the problem: to find something that we could share . . . it didn't really succeed. Maybe because of the age gap . . . maybe because of the difference between our educational approaches . . .

It is apparent that Sue assigns great value to the lounge. The explicit message in Sue's declaration is that she cannot enter the room. This is the difficulty that she expresses. In defining the teachers as a "bunch," she hints at the main difficulty in her perception of the problem: they are a closed and coherent group. The relevant adjacent phrase following the word "bunch" is the continuation of the statement:

> some of whom [the teachers] had taught me in the past,

In other words, there is a logical connection between the two parts of the sentence, through which we understand that the main barrier for Sue is of a personal nature. She apparently cannot shift from the state of being a student to relocate herself as a member of the teaching staff. Sue's case is particularly striking because she is teaching in the same school where she was a student. It might be that the physical entrance to the teachers' lounge awakens her tacit feeling of unease between her self-as-student and her self-as- teacher.

The age gap and difference in approaches that Sue refers to explicitly as her source of difficulty is another aspect of what she voices:

> I would think about things that were detached from what the teachers were talking about . . .

The veteran teachers, some of whom had taught her in the past, are far from her world and her way of thinking. Preferring to stay with the children, she distances herself from the staffroom.

The monologue suggests a kind of disappointment. Sue apparently expected from her veteran teachers, some of whom had probably been meaningful to her as a student, a different kind of hospitality and acceptance in the lounge. It seems that she was even looking forward to engaging with them in conversations about teaching and learning.

The struggle between alienation and closeness acquires a more emotionally loaded dimension in Olah's monologue, another novice teacher in her second year. She writes:

> What I am about to say is very sad but true! (at least that is how I feel). In my view, the lounge is not a "room" but a "space"! A public yard that is closed! Not only can teachers go in there but the principal can also go in at any time, and so can the janitor, the secretary and the parents (although there is a special room for that). And all sorts of *creatures* outside the teachers' territory can go inside!
>
> In the teachers' room there is constant gossiping and arguments, and one might say that the teachers

> don't want the arguments to end so that they will always have something to talk about!
>
> In short, it is not a comforting place but rather a distressing one! Even if there are many teachers that I would like to talk to at any moment . . . but as I've explained I don't have that opportunity.
>
> Teachers have no privacy ! and there are almost no advantages to the existence of a teachers' lounge!!!
>
> *(All the punctuation marks and emphases are in the original text).*

The new definition of the lounge as a closed, public, and distressing space for gossiping, explicitly describes Olah's attitude to the lounge. The importance of this description lies in her clear observation that, if the lounge is a territory meant only for the teachers, how is it that other people, such as secretaries, janitors, parents, and even the principal dare to invade it. There is also her view of the lounge as a territory that she does not belong to, for it is full of "creatures" who inhabit it.

The new perception of the lounge inherent in this monologue is the emotional declaration at the beginning of her monologue. The opening statements, accompanied by many exclamation marks, indicate her recurrent feelings of anger. Her way of using punctuation is an implicit signal that fits in nicely with Olah's explicit statement that all sorts of creatures invade the territory which she would like to see inhabited only by teachers. She would like the lounge to be a less crowded place with more privacy, in which case she would probably be able to find her own place within that territory.

In relation to Sue, who felt complete alienation from the lounge as a novice teacher and who also describes her need to "join" the lounge, Olah shows unmistakable signs of belonging to it in the very way that she complains about the fact that others occupy part of her territory. From her words we can hear a strong sense of criticism towards the basic situation created in the lounge—a gossiping situation. She declares that the place is not comforting but rather distressing and, in a very conclusive manner, adds

> Even if there are many teachers that I would like to talk to at any moment . . . but as I've explained I don't have that opportunity.

In other words, here, as with Sue, there is an implied longing for a sense of belonging. Olah would like to get closer to the teachers but she cannot find a way to do so, somewhat in the same manner that Sue did not find hers. Whereas Sue solved her problem by distancing herself from the lounge, at times staying closer to the children, Olah at this stage stays at a declarative level and does not take refuge in any "action." The many exclamation marks in the monologue leave no doubt that she is angry and disappointed because there is little she can do to change the situation.

During the interplay between reporting events and reflecting attitudes, Olah shares her views openly. She allows herself to express an explicitly detached attitude toward the lounge. She justifies her detachment from the lounge by reacting to the kind of talk that prevails in this territory, a kind of talk that is irrelevant and meaningless to her. She expresses a dichotomous emotional attitude: On the one hand, she sees no advantages to the lounge, which is very sad, and, on the other, that she is strongly attracted to this place as a potentially desirable space. This dichotomy is apparent in statements that were cited above from other monologues: "I hate to go into the lounge" vs. "I like the atmosphere in the lounge and I want to be there." This dichotomy runs through most of the monologues.

A different kind of monologue is what Rachel calls: "In place of a monologue." She chooses to write a list of seven elements to indicate her feelings about the lounge. The following is her list:

> gossiping
>
> obtuseness

"squareness"

lack of appraisal

conservatism

small talk

ventilation

The importance and innovation of what Rachel conveys lies not in the selection of elements with which she chooses to describe the lounge, but rather in the inner organization of the sequence in which these elements appear. Whether she does this consciously or unconsciously, she moves from the "heavy" to the "light," and from the undesirable to something that one might perhaps accept. All this of course is hinted at. At the explicit level, she decided to present a list without adding any descriptive details, reasons, or explanations. By composing a discourse of "signs" only, she has created a visual form of representing her experience. She enables us to enter her inner world through the form of her written monologue.

Regarding the first five items Rachel leaves us in no doubt that the connotation is negative. However, the last two, "small talk" and "ventilation," point to a direction that diverges from the view of the teachers' lounge as a hostile and detached place, to a more positive view of the lounge.

The contrasting and complex tendencies that have characterized the monologues until now converge into two statements in Orit's monologue. Orit wrote only:

> The teachers' lounge is a community characterized by a 'break without a break'. Break from the students - with the students.

Like Rachel, she uses a particular form of discourse to convey a definite attitude toward the teachers' lounge situation. This is construed through a paradoxical view of the controversial situations in the lounge. On the one hand, there are breaks in the school day, but these are not necessarily experienced as such by the teachers in the lounge. For teachers, one of the significant features of a break is a rest from dealing with students. But in Orit's view students are still a part of the lounge.

The following monologue by Anat summarizes and actually justifies this complex attitude towards the lounge. In contrast to other teachers, Anat presents from the beginning an explicitly positive attitude that defines her basic identification with the teachers' lounge. She perceives the lounge as an obviously important place within the culture of any school. As she writes about this space, she hints at its rough and unfriendly character, but diminishes the negative aspect by using a metaphor that is welcoming and comforting: that of the home. Her choice of metaphor emphasizes the two opposite poles of the continuum, i.e., alienation and belonging:

> The teachers' lounge is like a small home in which the family is nurtured. A family with many children, with one mother (the principal), a single-parent family. In this family there are:
>
> fights
>
> intimate talks
>
> advice
>
> support
>
> screams
>
> insults
>
> compromises
>
> celebrations
>
> sadness
>
> consultations
>
> A family with all the existing problems, the positive and negative sides but, as in any good family, everything stays indoors and you don't wash your dirty

> laundry outside and therefore when you go out of the lounge you pretend as though nothing happened and there are no problems. That is the lounge that I see.

This continuum of attraction and rejection, and of complex feelings toward the lounge, was especially salient in the novice teachers' monologues. They feel frustrated because they are willing but unable to penetrate the existing framework established by the veteran teachers in the lounge.

This point stresses the importance of the lounge and the necessity to address the issue in teacher education programs. It is important to prepare student teachers for similar "adult situations" they might encounter at school, in addition to preparing them for classroom situations. From the monologues it becomes clear that preparing and sensitizing student teachers to such affective and professional situations is necessary for their future induction into the community of discourse that develops in the teachers' lounge.

## Accepting the Nature of Lounges

A positive and more assertive approach to the lounge is shown by Sueher who discloses her world in the following monologue:

> When I went into the lounge for the first time I was very scared by the arguments that arose among teachers regarding the issue of "special benefits" to certain people in the Arab educational system. And they spoke all the time about those who could advance within the system not because of their potential and their great achievements but because they had some kind of support. This really scared me. But afterwards I joined in the group of teachers and spoke to one teacher who calmed me down and said that all this is not true. Little by little I understood that the lounge is a good place for intellectual discussions on any subject. The teachers talk, eat, and

> drink coffee. Personally I like this place because there is an atmosphere of partnership and peer work. But I heard that this partnership does not exist amongst all members of the staff and there are quarrels among different members as anywhere else. In conclusion, this is a good place. There are lots of journals and articles to read and there is a friendly atmosphere.

One of the characteristics of a coherent and flowing text is that the successive statements help the reader fill in gaps and assume that there are logical relations between parts of the sentence. For example, the relevant information that Sueher delivers is:

1. When I came into the lounge for the first time I was very scared.
2. But afterwards I joined in the group of teachers.

How did Sueher become part of this group? How did she manage to do what others could not? Does her monologue imply something about the process of induction into the lounge?

At the explicit level, Sueher conveys that she was very scared by the arguments that arose among teachers in the Arab sector regarding special benefits in the educational system. This information extends to her last sentence in which she establishes that the lounge is a good place with a friendly atmosphere. There is no logical connection between her scared feelings at the beginning of the monologue and the friendliness that she describes at the end. Her explanation that one teacher calmed her down is not substantial enough. Nevertheless, we implicitly understand that Sueher has a range of expectations about herself. She would like to develop and succeed in the educational system on the basis of her professional competence. Thus, possibly in order to dismiss her own lack of confidence, she assures herself that the lounge is, after all, a good place for talking and socializing. Still, she is ambivalent about this assertion and rephrases her statement later on by saying: "but I heard that this atmosphere does not exist among all members of the staff." But again, continuing to this statement, she reiterates: "there are quarrels among different members as anywhere else." This is in fact the most relevant utterance in her monologue. Sueher justifies the quarrels in the lounge by alluding to the general phenomenon of conflicts among adults. She argues that there is nothing one can do because this is the way relationships prevail in real life. At this stage we understand that the teacher who calmed her down at the beginning was not as important a factor as her own realization that these kind of dynamics among people are universal and characteristic of any adult society. Since she feels at peace with this assertion, she is ready to state explicitly that the teachers' lounge is a desirable place.

It is not difficult to understand Sueher's position. She expresses what previous monologues have revealed along the continuum of rejection and attraction. In her case, though, the pole of attraction is more prominent.

## Struggling with the "Former Student" Syndrome

Amira opens her monologue as follows:

> I remember the lounge in the Junior High School where I studied. It was a small and crowded room. Many teachers would stand on the side or outside the room during break. As a student I had many opportunities to go into the lounge when I had to arrange things with other teachers, and especially with my homeroom teacher. I don't know whether this was just a feeling of a high school student who is timid and not aware of what happens over there with the teachers—"the monsters." With all my innocence as a student I felt in a hostile and uncomfortable atmosphere. I sensed tense relations among the teachers, especially a hostile attitude towards the principal who would, occasionally, go in to hand out

> materials. Now I am a university graduate and visit several schools during the week and I look differently at the tensions between the teachers . . .

The memory of the lounge as recalled by a student is an important theme that occurs in sixty percent of the monologues. The teachers raise, in one way or another, their memory of the lounge when they were students. This indicates their need to redefine their present perspective of the lounge through the prism of their past experience as students. This comparative dimension is important for our understanding of lounges. Amira writes about herself as a student: at that time, she saw in the teachers' lounge a strange body of people, or "monsters." Although it is clear that the use of the word "monsters" in quotation marks suggests a metaphorical use, it still conveys the notion of the teachers' world as a closed and frightening place. From her innocent point of view as a student, the lounge looks small, crowded, and full of tensions. Today, as a teacher, Amira understands and explains the tensions in the lounge: they result from the shortness of the breaks, five to ten minutes, during which there is a lot to do.

Amira's way of coping with the tensions in the lounge is by recalling her memories of the lounge as a student, and using these memories to provide a new understanding of her life in the same room as a teacher.

We can find a similar pattern in Ruth's monologue:

> In my first days at school I felt embarrassment in the lounge. At the beginning, there were still some silly feelings of a student coming in to a forbidden territory. Afterward, when I saw students hesitating in front of the door, it looked so illogical to view the lounge as "sacred." In the meeting with the students, and in my relationship with them, this separation looked to me arbitrary and egoistic. On the other hand I enjoy the few minutes in which I can relax a bit and enjoy the break . . .

Her feelings toward the lounge emanate from her schoolgirl memory of the lounge, painting an image of a distanced and almost "sacred" place. For Ruth, it is important that her students feel comfortable enough to cross the borders of the lounge. She thinks that it is egoistic not to allow them in. But she also expresses explicitly her pleasure in the few times she can be alone in the lounge without any students around her. In this way, she hints at the important function of the room as a territory that belongs primarily to the teachers.

## Concluding Comments

This chapter reflects the way teachers experience lounges and think about them as exhibiting contradictory features.

We asked teachers a direct question to elicit their metaphors concerning lounges. These allowed us to sketch a map of their manifold ways of relating to their lounges. Similarly, the teachers' monologues revealed their opposing views toward lounges.

The strong feelings that emerge from the teachers' monologues testify to the importance of such a place and its centrality in their life. It is by no means a neutral place. Therefore, it is important to pay attention and inquire into the various events that take place there. The wide-ranging attitudes toward the lounge indicate its different professional and social functions. The teachers' accounts of the lounge as reflecting the "former student" syndrome is an important point of reference in the relationship between open and closed lounges. It reveals the essence of reciprocal relationships between teachers and students, here expressed outside the classrooms.

The voices of the teachers discerned through the metaphors and monologues reflect a wide and complex variety of discourses. These encompass contrasting and ambivalent perceptions of teachers' professional identity, socialization processes, and the daily functions of the lounge in their lives.

Toulmin (1980) argues that:

> A properly evolutionary way of dealing with experience obliges us to recognize that no event or process has any single unambiguous description: we describe any event in different terms, and view it as an element in a different network of relations, depending on the standpoint from which—and the purposes for which—we are considering it. (p.38)

Jackson (1986) claims that teaching, as well, could be located within a network of relations. The teachers' lounge is an appropriate place where these networks can develop.

## CHAPTER 6

# Teachers' Perception of Lounges and Student Achievement (coauthored with Haggai Kupermintz)

This chapter focuses on the relationships between organizational and experiential elements of teachers' communities in the lounge, on the one hand, and student achievement, on the other hand. What specific conditions in the lounge might foster, or conversely hinder, the development of professional communities of teachers? How are these conditions associated with student achievement?

Teachers' perceptions of the characteristics, functions, and spheres of influences of their lounges, as well as the relationship between these perceptions and students' academic achievement are at the heart of this chapter. It is important to emphasize that teachers' lounges are part of the social reality of teachers, particularly in Israel. The study of teachers' perceptions of their lounges is based on two assumptions:

(a) The teachers' lounge is a regular meeting place for people who share common interests, and who expect to develop professional relationships.
(b) Teachers' participation in the various activities of the lounge is determined by their need to cooperate with their colleagues, and is not compulsory.

This chapter is based on an empirical study of nineteen Israeli elementary schools. We start with an analysis of teachers' perceptions of their lounges. The second part of the chapter focuses on the relationship between these perceptions and students' performance on achievement tests conducted in these schools. We discuss the possible implications of the relationships found in the study. This discussion leads to an attempt to deal with the questions raised at the beginning of this chapter. Details of the design and structure of this part of our study of lounges were presented in the first chapter.

## Demographic and School Background Data

The study reported in this chapter was part of a larger survey conducted in nineteen elementary, mostly urban, schools in Israel. Four hundred and nine elementary school teachers (95 percent female) responded to the teacher's lounge questionnaire. Teachers in the study had on the average twelve years of teaching experience and seven years of experience in their current school. Most teachers reported a five-day work week during which they typically visited their lounges more than twice a day. The actual time teachers spend in the lounge exceeds one hour (three recesses), and may in fact be more whenever teachers have an unscheduled free period.

## Teachers' Lounges Questionnaire

A self-report questionnaire was constructed, on the basis of preliminary interviews with teachers, to gauge their perceptions of their lounges. The questionnaire was composed of two parts:

(a) Teachers were asked to indicate the appropriateness of twenty characteristics to describing their own lounge (for example, "noisy"; "pleasant atmosphere"; "competitive environment"; "a place to prepare lessons" ; "a place to talk with students"). Responses were measured on a 5–point scale, ranging from "not true or very seldom true for the teachers' lounge in my school" to "very often true for the teachers' lounge in my school."

(b) Teachers were asked to assess the perceived impact of teachers' lounges on ten school-related domains (e.g., "improving school climate"; "developing interpersonal relationships between teachers"; "developing educational activities"). Responses were measured on 5-point scale ranging from "no impact" to "great impact."

The questionnaire also included an open-ended part in which the participating teachers were asked to elaborate on some of their experiences in the lounge and to offer metaphors which described their lounge.

## The Perceived Characteristics of Teachers' Lounges

We first explored the questionnaire by examining the structure of correlations among teacher responses to specific items. The statistical technique of factor analysis provided a useful summary of responses by clustering items into meaningful groups (factors). Items to which teachers tended to respond in the same way (thus exhibiting high correlations) were placed in the same cluster. Three such item-clusters, describing the characteristics of the teacher lounge, emerged from the analysis of the first section of the questionnaire. The item clusters are presented in Table 1.

Based on the arrangement of the various characteristics, these item-clusters can be best interpreted in terms of the three distinct functions that teachers attribute to their lounge. The *social function* depicts the communal rather than the professional dimension of the teachers' lounge. The perceived atmosphere is pleasant and colorful, and the lounge is described as a place to relax and socialize with one's colleagues. In this context, visits from the principal, and the communication of information, likely pertain to social interactions. The lounge's social function is exemplified by Dana's comments in one of the interviews:

**Table 1. Item clusters of teachers' lounge characteristics**

| |
|---|
| Social function: |
| Pleasant atmosphere |
| Expansive, lots of space |
| A great deal of information communicated |
| Humor |
| Colorful |
| The principal drops in |
| Tolerance |
| A place to talk with colleagues |
| A place to rest |
| Political function: |
| Noisy |
| Overflowing with students |
| Competitive environment |
| Regular seating arrangement |
| Leadership is established |
| Sharing of secrets |
| Professional competitiveness |
| Work function: |
| Lessons are prepared |
| Tests are graded |
| A place to talk with parents |
| A place to talk with students |

> I am totally convinced that for teachers, school becomes a second home. Teacher's work at school deals mainly with emotions and the teachers' lounge offers them support and serves as a place where one can laugh or cry without anyone interfering.

The *political function*, in a marked distinction from the social function, describes the lounge as part of the stressful and challenging reality of the profession. The lounge is perceived as a place where professional power struggles are played out, characterized by competitiveness, secrecy, and the establishment of leadership. Regular seating arrangements likely reflect the hierarchy structure among teachers. Power struggles in the lounge can cause great pain, as is the case of Sarah (which we presented in chapter 4):

Sarah was celebrating the wedding of her daughter who was a graduate of the school. She was so relaxed that she admitted that she was "fed up with working. I'm ready to retire, and help bring up my own grandchildren." Ron, a school executive responded: "The students will happily agree with you." The peaceful atmosphere immediately changed. Sarah controlled her anger and hurt but became tense. Her friend tried to save the situation by loudly joking: "Of course the students would be happy if all of us retired." Teachers began to laugh. They continued eating and talking as usual, but it was clear that for Sarah the intimacy of the teachers' lounge was lost, as was the sense of belonging to the community.

The *work function* describes the teachers' lounge as a place to carry out professional duties. Teachers in Israel typically do not have their own offices, and therefore use the lounge to meet with students and parents, and to prepare for lessons or correct exams. The lounge appears to facilitate professional community building through cooperation and sharing of professional tasks. The informal environment opens opportunities for teachers to form ad hoc collaborations geared toward specific tasks, such as the preparation of a school commemoration day. Jane, in one of our interviews cited above in chapter 4, reveals an interesting interplay between the social and work functions of the teachers' lounge:

> There is a great paradox in this matter of lounges. On [the] one hand, it is a place to relax in, away from work; we enter the lounge to "clean our heads," but if we listen to what we are talking about there, we can clearly see that only a few of us are not talking about work. It is rare that the subject is about anything but work. In fact we continue working even during our

> free periods, and despite this we love being there. I don't know how to explain it; however, I feel that I rest, even though I am working.

Our analysis suggests that teachers simultaneously ascribe multiple functions to their lounge, portraying a picture of a complex public space—a place to socialize and relax, to engage in internal politics, and to carry out professional duties. The intricate and often conflicting realities of the teaching profession are clearly reflected in this picture.

A closer look at teachers' responses, however, reveals that the different functions do not have equal power in portraying the prominent feature of the teachers' lounge. Teachers' reports on how much each characteristic is adequate to describe their school's lounge indicate that the social function describes the lounge much better than the other two functions. The average rating for characteristics associated with the lounge's social function was 3.7, compared to average ratings of 2.2 and 2.3 for the political and work functions characteristics, respectively. That is, according to teachers' responses, the social function was "often" an adequate description of their lounge, while the political and work functions were "sometimes" or even "seldom" adequate descriptions. Teachers, therefore, perceive their lounge first and foremost as a place for social interaction with their peers, a place where one can relax in a pleasant atmosphere and have supportive exchanges with colleagues. This finding may also reflect a tendency of women to attribute much importance to interpersonal relations. The lesser emphasis on the political and work functions is meaningful but should not be interpreted as indicating only a negligible role for these functions. The reality of the teachers' lounge is very complicated, and the political and work functions are potent and powerful elements in determining the nature and atmosphere of interactions in the lounge, as demonstrated by events presented throughout this book.

Teachers' responses portray their sense of the reality of lounges, what they are, what they are not, and what they could be. When competing demands of teachers' professional lives and differences in professional and personal preferences exist, the delicate balance of the teachers' lounge functions is brought to the forefront or even challenged. The lounge then becomes a stage for high drama of intricate interpersonal interactions; some are explicit, while many others are indirect and subtle.

The distinction among the different functions is often blurred in the concrete, existential, ongoing, and shifting situations in teachers' lounges. However, beyond the kaleidoscopic events in teachers' lounges, the various aspects of their functions might become dominant at different times during the school day or school year. Schools follow temporal cycles—annual, monthly, weekly—which, according to Connelly and Clandinin (1990), determine a characteristic sequence of events involving teachers, students, administrators, and support staff. The shifting functions of the teachers' lounge can be viewed through these temporal cycles.. The introduction of an innovative curriculum may bring to the forefront the lounge's work function. Before the end of the school day the lounge may turn into an arena of social interactions. And when a new principal is appointed, the political function of the lounge may become most pronounced.

Because we are interested in the culture of teachers' lounges as a part of the overall school culture, and not as an isolated realm, we turn now to teachers' perceptions of the influence of lounges on life in schools.

## Spheres of Perceived Influence of Lounges on Life in Schools

When asked about the influence of the teachers' lounge on their school, teachers made few distinctions among the different aspects of impact. This was rather surprising given the number of topics covered in the questionnaire: the topics ranged from addressing peer relations to dealing with students and the principal. Nevertheless, the intensity of the overall perceived influence of the lounge could still be measured and the average rating for the influence items was 3.5, which indicates that teachers perceive their lounge to have "certain" or "considerable" influence on school life.

Examining the relationships between perceived influence and the three lounge functions revealed a strong positive correlation with the social function but no correlations with the political or work functions. In other words, teachers who view the lounge as a place to relax and to engage in positive social interactions with colleagues, also view it as a considerable source of influence on school life in general. This finding underscores the importance of the affective dimension of teachers' worklife. The social context may be thought to constitute a prerequisite for the formation of a professional community of teachers and, in turn, lead to the development of a sense of efficacy and potency with regard to various aspects of school life. The characteristics of the lounge's social function portray an unthreatening atmosphere which promotes teacher networking and teaming. Teachers' interactions with their colleagues and with the principal in a restful, tolerant, and pleasant environment play an important role in providing a set of conditions which create links between the lounge and school events. We have seen above how professional issues are interwoven in the fabric of the social interactions in the lounge. Such exchanges, when accompanied by an atmosphere of collegial trust and support, might help teachers to reshape and examine their professional identities and, in turn, have a direct influence on classroom practice.

Just as important is the lack of correlation between the political and work functions and the perceived influence of the lounge on school life. While the social function is directly associated with the impact teachers ascribe to the lounge in their workplace, the "harsher" aspects of the lounge's characteristics are not perceived as inhibiting factors to its influence. One may have reasonably expected that the overall atmosphere which marks the political function—noisy, competitive, secretive, and hierarchical—would have negative influence on school life. Conflicts and dilemmas which are apt to rise in such environments could have been perceived by teachers as prohibitive to the positive influence of the lounge on improving interpersonal relationships, or on creating professional cooperation. The empirical evidence, however, does not confirm such expectations.

When teachers try to reflect upon the influence their lounges have on school life, the primary reference point is the extent to which the lounge promotes social interactions among themselves. Acknowledging the existence of tougher and sometimes unpleasant aspects of life in the lounge does not seem to be a chief concern in terms of the lounges' importance to the larger context of school life. It is possible that the community-building nature of the social function is weighted heavily as a crucial component for exerting influence throughout the school, while the more negative or counterproductive elements of lounge life are perceived as an inevitable evil, and for the most part a natural aspect of any human interaction. Later, we shall present a more detailed account of the relationships between the teaches lounge's functions and specific areas of influence on school life.

## Teachers' Lounges and Students' Achievement

Our purpose in this section is to investigate the relationships between the perceptions teachers hold with respect to their lounge's functions, its influence on school life, and their students' achievement.

Average achievement on standardized tests in math and in reading comprehension, administered by the Ministry of Education in grades 3 and 5 in all elementary schools in Israel, was available for each school in the study. Based on test scores (averaged across the two subjects), schools were divided into two groups: low-achieving and high-achieving, according to their relative standing below or above the overall average test scores in the sample. In low-achieving schools (8 schools, 181 teachers) the average failure rate was 42 percent, while in high-achieving schools (11 schools, 228 teachers) the failure rate was 14 percent. The two groups of schools were quite comparable with respect to size, teacher-to-student ratio, and physical characteristics, such as relative classroom space per student.

Two questions guided our analyses in this section: a) are there differences between teachers in low- and high-achieving schools in their perceptions of the teachers' lounge functions and influence? and b) how do teachers in low- and high-achieving schools associate the teachers' lounge functions with specific domains of influence on school life?

In order to answer the first question, we compared the average ratings of the three lounge functions and the lounge's influence on school life in low- and high-achieving schools. Figure 1 presents these average scores by school achievement level.

Figure 1 shows that teachers in high-achieving schools perceive the characteristics of the social function as a more appropriate description of their lounge than do their low-achieving school counterparts. They also perceive the lounge to be a more influential source on school life. The political and work functions were perceived as much less characteristic of the teachers' lounges by teachers in schools from both achievement levels.

The perceived prominence of the social function and the influence of the lounge on school life among teachers in high-achieving schools supports the hypothesis that a strong teacher community has a positive impact on student achievement. However, a conclusive causal interpretation of these findings is unwarranted. The substantial differences in school culture and climate between low- and high-achieving schools likely reflect a complex set of reciprocal influences between teachers and students. Teachers in schools where students are generally doing well might be able to devote more time and energy to cultivate interpersonal relationships with one another and spend their time in the lounge mainly for relaxing, socializing, and having productive discussions on personal or professional matters. In turn, they perceive the teachers' lounge as an important source of influence on the entire school. In contrast, in schools where student achievement is low, teachers' re-

**Figure 1.** Teachers' Lounge Functions and Influence by School Achievement Level

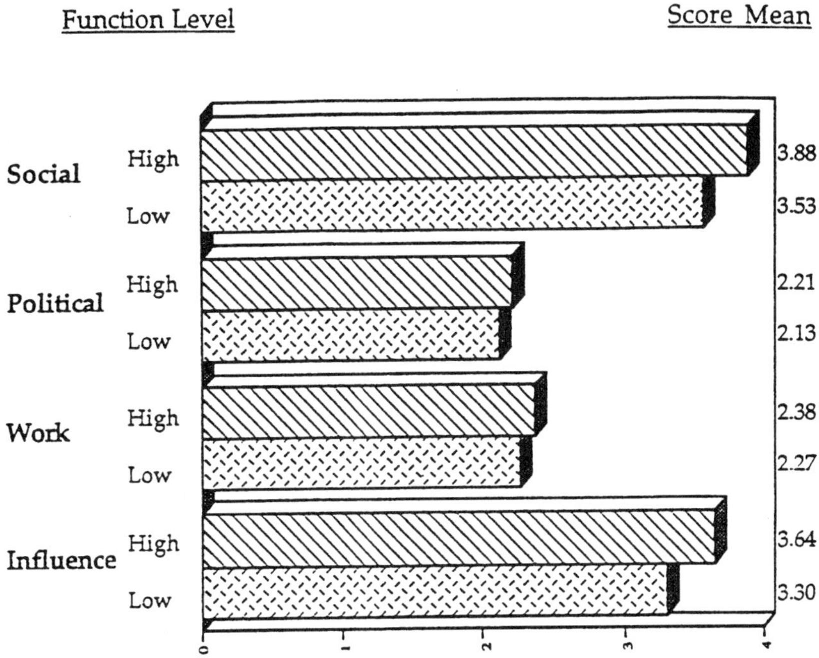


High – stands for high-achievement schools
Low – stands for low-achievement schools

sponses indicate a weaker sense of community regarding their lounge experience, characterized by less, or even a lack of, opportunity for spending relaxed social time together in the lounge. It is interesting, however, that the same teachers do not report more emphasis on the political function, again suggesting the social realm as the more important point of reference.

To investigate the links between the perceived functions of teachers' lounges, and their influence on school life, we looked at the relationships between each function and the ten items describing specific domains of influence of the teachers' lounge on school life. Although the specific items sum up to reflect a general influence factor, it was considered important to examine them separately in order to shed more light on the differences between low- and high-achieving schools.

Overall, the social function was strongly associated with influence on professional cooperation, communication channels, interpersonal relations, and school climate, supporting the interpretation of the social function offered earlier, as reflecting an emphasis on interpersonal relations and communication among teachers. It is clear that a supportive atmosphere in the teachers' lounge is associated for most teachers, regardless of their school's academic achievement, with an enhanced quality of professional and personal relations in school.

Stronger relationships were found between the social function and influence items for teachers in low-achieving schools. The difference in the magnitude of correlations was especially pronounced for influence on treatment of individual students, on relations between teachers and the principal, and on raising motivation for work. In contrast to teachers in low-achieving schools, teachers in the high-achieving schools did not associate influence in these domains with the social function of the teachers' lounge. These results pose a seemingly puzzling pattern because of the overall stronger emphasis of teachers in high-achieving schools on the social function.

The strong association between the lounge's social function and its influence on school life in low-achieving schools may be best understood by considering a possible deficiency in such schools of established and effective ways to deal with individual students and their needs. In these schools, the relations between teachers and principals might be strained, and there might be a generalized feeling of teacher burn-out. Under such circumstances, the social function of the teachers' lounge could become extremely important in mitigating such limitations. Thus, for teachers who experience an unpleasant, and many times unfriendly and hostile workplace, a positive and supportive teachers' lounge holds special value. The contrast of such a place to other aspects of professional life in low-achieving schools might contribute to the lounge's perceived importance as an enabling force.

What teachers in high-achieving schools accept as the norm cannot be taken for granted by teachers in low-achieving schools. It can reasonably be argued that for many of these teachers, the lounge is one of the only places in their work environment with the potential to offer a sense of cooperation, sharing, and encouragement, which in turn contributes to its perceived influence on other aspects of school life.

For teachers in low-achieving schools there were also negative correlations between the political function and the perceived influence of the lounge on dealing with professional issues, and professional cooperation. We suggested above that professional competition may be considered a natural part of the professional climate in school, and, as such, its manifestations in the teachers' lounge do not inhibit the overall influence of the lounge on school life. While this overall pattern holds, in seems that, in low-achieving schools, manifestations of professional competitiveness in the teachers' lounge might be interpreted as insurmountable obstacles in the daily work of the school. Again, we see that, for these teachers, events that take place in the lounge are echoed in broader school domains. Professional cooperation among teachers and effective problem-solving mechanisms are likely to be sensitive, and often painful issues in low-achieving schools, so that overt threats to them in the teachers' lounge are more readily viewed as symptomatic of the entire school culture, resulting in poorer management of professional problems and weaker collaborations among colleagues.

Only for teachers in high-achieving schools, was the work function of the teachers' lounge found to be associated with influence on the treatment of individual students, and in dealing with professional issues. A possible explanation for this finding is that low-achieving schools lack the kind of professional work climate which characterizes the life of teachers in high-achieving schools. Because their work environment is not learning-enriched (Rosenholtz 1989), teachers in low-achieving schools may not perceive specific links between lounges and professional growth, or professional activities, such as treatment of individual students.

We saw earlier that for these teachers the professional domain is influenced more by the intensity of the political function of the teachers' lounge. Teachers in high-achieving schools, on the other hand, are able to identify the benefits of productive professional activities in the lounge, especially for promoting communication with, and treatment of, individual students.

Overall, it seems that teachers in high-achievement schools are better able to differentiate between the teachers' lounge functions in terms of their influence on various aspects of school life. They associate the social function mainly with influence on the interpersonal-relations dimension, and the work function with the appropriate aspects of their professional activities. On the other hand, teachers from low-achieving schools tend to give an omnibus interpretation to the effects of the social functions of the teachers' lounge to encompass professional, as well as interpersonal domains. At the same time they perceive displays of professional competitiveness as constraining factors of the lounges' influence.

## Concluding Comments

The study described in this chapter provides insights into the ways in which teachers perceive an important aspect of their workplace and how these perceptions might be linked to student learning outcomes. Through the uncovering of the importance teachers assign to the social function of lounges we gained an understanding of the conditions in which communities of teachers develop. Especially important in this context is the difference between teachers in high- and low-achieving schools concerning the functions of their lounges, which are viewed as serving the social functions more in high-achieving schools. This finding supports the arguments of Talbert and McLaughlin (1994) about the important role that institutional factors play in establishing teacher professionalism through social interactions. The perceived power of the social elements of life in teachers' lounges seems to extend over the work function and to subsume it. Teachers' professional development, as members in a community of practice, takes place in a social environment and depends on social interactions. The natural site for these interactions in the workplace is the teachers' lounge.

Some of the specific conditions of school organization which might foster the development of strong professional communities of teachers through social interactions in the teachers' lounge are noted by teachers in our study. Their interviews and responses to the questionnaire indicate that the social function of their lounges is determined both by physical aspects of space and color, as well as by affective aspects such as tolerance and humor, and by providing opportunities to rest, to talk with colleagues, and to share information.

Teachers' perceptions of their lounges, and the role lounges play, are closely linked to, and possibly dependent on, the school context. High-achieving schools constitute a positive workplace, with an emphasis on social interactions in the lounge, and a positive awareness of its overall influence on school life. The relations between teachers' perceptions of their lounges and student achievement are likely reciprocal.

A more intensely social function of lounges, through enabling and facilitating teachers' professionalism, might lead to high achievement, and higher achievement, in turn, might strengthen the social function of the lounge. These potential patterns are presented schematically in Figure 2, which highlights some important components of this process. Furthermore, consistent with these reciprocal links between the nature of interactions in the lounge and student achievement, teachers in high-achieving schools experience their lounge as a potent source of influence on school life.

In low-achieving schools, conditions that hinder the development of powerful communities of teachers are reflected in the perceptions of teachers' lounges. As noted above, negative correlations were found for teachers in low-achieving schools between the political, competitive function of their lounges and the perceived influence of the lounge on dealing with professional issues. Here too, we suggest a reciprocal

**Figure 2.** A model for describing the relationship between teachers' perception of their lounge and student achievement

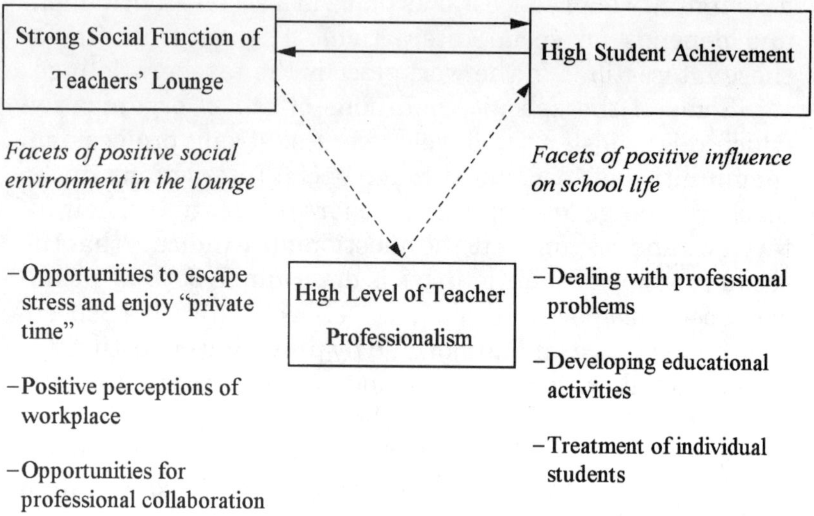


Note: The solid-line arrows reflect the empirical finding of the correlation between perception of the social function and student achievement. The broken-line arrows refer to the process behind the empirical correlation.

relationship between the political function of the lounge and student achievement. The more competitive and less accepting the lounge is, the smaller the chances are for establishing a productive professional community of teachers, resulting in lower student achievement. On the other hand, low student achievement might lead to high levels of political competitiveness in the lounge coupled with a perception of limited influence of teachers' experiences in their lounge on professional aspects of school life.

Our study highlights the importance of teachers' lounges in facilitating the process of professional development and its potential contribution to student achievement. Trying to break the mold of competitiveness in the teachers' lounge and to promote the formation of an environment of positive social interactions might serve the establishment of professional communities of teachers in schools.

CHAPTER 7

# Principals in the Teachers' Lounge: Intruders or Colleagues?

How school principals fit into the picture was described in the previous chapters. What role do they play in this context? What is the relationship between the leadership styles of principals and their behavior in the lounge? And, last but not least, how do teachers react to the visits of principals to the lounge? Do teachers behave differently, just as students change their behavior when the teacher enters the class?

In order to answer these questions, twelve principals were selected at random from the district of Haifa. Four were principals of elementary schools, four of junior high schools, and four of senior high schools. It is interesting to note that eleven principals were women, and only one, a high school principal, was a man. This phenomenon reflects the sharp increase of women in leadership positions in education.

Over two months, teachers' rooms were observed and videotaped, and teachers were interviewed. Documents such as announcements made by principals were collected. All these materials were analyzed leading to several insights concerning the nature of principals' involvement in the teachers' lounge.

## Principals' Involvement in the Lounge

An assumption of our research is that teachers' lounges constitute a central channel of communication between principals and teachers. In the informal climate of the lounge, principals convey direct or indirect messages reflecting their modes of management, and their style of collaboration with teachers.

The rhythm of life in school is governed by the bell. The recurring cycles of lessons and breaks create opportunities for intended or unplanned interactions between principals and teachers. Four time spaces during the school day present such opportunities: (a) the beginning of the school day—the entry phase when teachers may congregate in the lounge, before entering their classes; (b) the end of the school day—the exit phase, when teachers can spend some time in the lounge before returning home; (c)during breaks between lessons—the rings of the bell phase; and (d) the longest time space—the free time phase, which teachers might have during the day.

It is important to note that the nature of the lounge differs for principals and for teachers. While the lounge might serve mainly as a "backstage" territory for teachers, who are in need of some "private time," it serves usually as another "frontstage" domain for principals, who are acting in their "public time." Only rarely do principals enter the lounge just for a cup of coffee, or for a moment of leisure: usually they have some mission to accomplish. The dissonance between these different aspects of time and space might cause dilemmas and conflicts, and reflects the blurring of boundaries in the lounge.

One might characterize the forms of principals' involvement in the lounge as having two aspects. One, the behavioral aspect, relates to the frequency of principals' visits to the lounge. The other, the motivational aspect, relates to their motives for entering the lounge; they might be social or professional.

## The Frequency of Principals' Visits to the Lounge

The principals in our study were asked to describe their daily interactions with teachers and the frequency of their visits to the teachers' lounge. All the principals stated that they enter the lounge every day. Each described this routine differently, for instance:

- I try to be in the lounge at least during one break every day.
- I like to enter the lounge at the end of the day. The pressures and strains of the day are over and one can talk at ease.
- I organize my day in such a way that I spend the long break in the lounge.
- I am usually in the lounge during free lessons time, when only a few teachers stay in the lounge and I can talk with them.
- I enter the lounge frequently. It is situated near my office, therefore I almost always go there for delivering different announcements. I also enter the lounge after the breaks, when the teachers have left for their classrooms, and see to it that the room stays clean and tidy.

The statements of principals reflect their individual preferences for different temporal choices in their visits to the lounge. These choices express their motivations for being in the lounge, such as quiet conversations with individual teachers, or sharing official announcements with the whole staff. While some principals might choose to spend the long break with the teachers, possibly implying their sense of belonging to their community, others might express their commitment to the staff through caring for the physical aspects of their room.

To our question whether they could imagine their school without a teachers' lounge, all principals replied unequivocally that they considered the room to be an indispensable component of schools. They expressed this view in different ways

- No, never. The reason is simple, a school without a teachers' lounge is bound to be a school with no sense of community.

- No, I could not imagine my school without this important place, which has no substitute.
- The teachers' lounge is the most important room in the school. The atmosphere in the lounge reflects the success or failure of the school administration. The ethos and mission of the school are expressed in the teachers' lounge.

One principal commented about a period of time when the lounge at her school was closed for three years due to changes in the school building:

- I can't understand how we managed all this time without a lounge.

## Leadership Styles of Principals and their Expression in the Lounge

The principals in our study viewed the lounge as important for the management of successful schools. How do they facilitate this goal through their involvement in the lounge?

Hall & Rutherford (1983) distinguished between three styles of principals' leadership in facilitating school improvement: responder, manager, and initiator. The **responder style** of management is characterized by a view of teachers as autonomous professionals; the principal who acts as a responder, therefore, tends not to intervene in the daily practice of teachers. Decisions tend to be made in response to specific situations arising in the context of schooling. Close personal relationships with teachers are considered very important. The main motivation of principals with a responder style of management for involvement in the lounge might, therefore, be social. The "responding" principal tends to visit the lounge often and assigns great importance to his/her relationships with teachers. These principals state:

- It is very important for me that the atmosphere in the lounge be pleasant.

- I feel that I have to do everything so that the atmosphere will be good.
- I want the teachers to feel that I am one of them.

The "responding" principal mingles with teachers in the lounge and is open to and supportive of their questions and ideas. According to this approach:

> The teachers' lounge is a source of oxygen for teachers who spend much energy in their work. They know their profession and have a strong need to fortify themselves. The teachers' lounge fulfills this need and has to be suitable for this function.

This kind of principal wants to feel close to the teachers:

> As a good principal, I like to enter the lounge and see everyone talk, laugh, and drink coffee.

Sometimes principals will feel alien in the lounge, when teachers are involved in activities that exclude them:

> During the break I entered the lounge as usual. Everyone was busy with elections for the teachers' union. I felt superfluous.

This style of management might cause dilemmas in the lounge:

> During the long break I was in the teachers' lounge. One teacher entered with a large box of chocolates, celebrating his engagement. The teachers started to quote poetry, they drank coffee, and everyone had a wonderful time. When the bell rang no one rose to go to the classroom. How does one break up such a pleasant mood? In such moments I do not know whether I am a teacher or a principal.

This role dilemma of "responding" principals reflects the gap between the "backstage" nature of the lounge from the point of view of teachers, and the role requirements of principals, who are expected to perform "frontstage," using their authority.

The more open the principal is, the more pressing this dilemma becomes, raising the question of how close should principals get to their teachers. Sometimes this dilemma creates a sense of failure and loss:

> When I enter the lounge I find myself on duty. I miss the heart-to-heart conversations I had with my colleagues when I myself was a teacher.

What is the price one has to pay for giving priority to the social aspects of the relationship between teachers, and between principals and teachers? The following episode exemplifies this problem:

> Last year one of the teachers got a divorce. Everyone supported her. This was very positive but disrupted the regular functioning of the school. Her colleagues were involved in giving support and she was engaged in her problems. The teachers did not leave the lounge on time for their classes because of long conversations with her. When I grasped this situation I knew I had to do something about it but did not know how to act. The teachers' lounge should be a place for relaxation and social interaction, but at what price?

The **manager-style** of principals is characterized by an organizational approach. The manager-style principals communicate their decisions to teachers: they tend to support change, especially when initiated by the establishment. Manager-style principals tend to enter the lounge in the context of tasks to be accomplished, and are more oriented towards these tasks than towards interpersonal relationships. Though sensitive to the needs of teachers, they will hesitate to intervene personally:

> I entered the teachers' lounge. It was 7.45 a.m. The first thing I noticed was that one of the teachers was

> sitting far from his usual place. I wanted to ask what had happened but thought it was none of my business.
>
> In our school there are several breaks, not all teachers share the same breaks. Sometimes I enter the lounge and find two teachers engaged in conversation. I leave and do not interfere.

In spite of this expressed sensitivity to the privacy of teachers, it is important for manager-style principals to have their opinions communicated to teachers:

> The teachers' union had declared a strike. As every school event is dealt with in the teachers' lounge, I went there to clarify that this time I agreed with their perspective.

Manager-style principals are always around; their role dilemma has to do with the issue of time. Manager-style principals perceive their time in school as "public time" and expect the same of teachers, causing a blurring of boundaries for teachers who might perceive their time in the lounge as "private time." The lounges in their schools are characterized by large amounts of information communicated to teachers, orally and in writing, in the teachers' mailboxes, and through announcements on the walls.

**Initiator-style** principals tend to lead school improvement and have high expectations of teachers, students, and of themselves. In everyday interactions the initiators tend to be businesslike; therefore, their visits to the teachers' lounge are determined by their perception of the lounge as instrumental for the achievement of school goals:

> Two years ago I was a new principal, new in the school and new as principal. Visits to the teachers' lounge were very difficult for me. I did not know what to do there. Today, after two years, it seems to me that I erred when I tried to be friendly with teachers during breaks. This was not my style. The teachers'

> lounge is a workplace, it is an instrument I have to get to know.

Initiator-style principals view the lounge as a place for professional activities, and for communicating their wishes and demands:

> I entered the lounge and told everyone that, because of the external examinations taking place on the following day, all teachers would have to be present at school, even those who had a free day, in order to facilitate the organization of the exams.

Because of their focus on professional activities, initiator-style principals are not ambiguous about the role of the teachers' lounge, and do not perceive any blurring of boundaries concerning its function:

> The teachers' lounge is not a "backstage" area for me or for the teachers. I would have liked, of course, that there would also be a quiet corner in school, but the teachers' lounge is a workplace for all . . .

Such a principal organizes the school timetable in such a way that free periods of teachers can serve for collaborative work,

> I try to arrange simultaneous free periods for teachers in a specific subject area. I have, for instance, a team who teach social studies. Their common free period in the lounge has become an hour of shared work. From time to time I enter the lounge during that time and join in these informal meetings.

As principals experience the nature of life in the lounge, these experiences might have a subtle influence on their own modes of leadership. If, for instance, principals who want to feel close to their teachers (such as the one who stated that she liked to enter the lounge and see everyone talking and laughing) have the opportunity to be present when the lounge functions as a site for professional work, then their own perspective might change to include some of the more businesslike components of manager-style principals.

Change might also work in the opposite direction, with manager-style or initiator-style principals becoming more open to social interactions in the lounge, viewing the lounge not only as a workplace, but also as a place for creating a community of teachers. Gender might play an important role in the interactions between principals and teachers in the lounge. Male principals could find the situation in the lounge threatening their leadership function and try to establish their dominance in various ways.

Case studies of principals who held leadership positions in various schools could provide insights into the impact of the cultures of teachers' lounges on management styles.

## Teachers' Reactions to the Visits of Principals to the Lounge

What are teachers' reactions to the different modes of interactions with their principals in the teachers' lounge? Are principals regarded by teachers as intruders into "their" space, or do they become colleagues sharing a common place and time?

Teachers were asked to comment on the visits of principals to the lounge. It seems that their reactions to the entrance of the principal into the lounge are similar to students' reactions when a teacher comes into the classroom; there is a change of atmosphere and behavior.

One teacher, with twenty-three years of experience, who had worked with three different principals, said:

> The entrance of the principal creates stress, and it is difficult to understand why this is so.

No matter how relaxed and pleasant the atmosphere in the staffroom may be, it is inevitable that the entrance of the principal will change it. This impression has been noted in all our observations in lounges, apart from two cases. One was the teachers' lounge in "an open school" and the other was at an art school where the principal was regarded as an integral part of the teaching staff. In most cases, however, when the principal enters the teachers' lounge, teachers feel uneasy. We might interpret this feeling as originating in the communal knowledge of teachers; according to this communal wisdom, the principal is perceived as a supervisor and ongoing evaluator. Riva states that:

> there are principals whose entrance results in a growing tension in the atmosphere.

A new teacher argues that

> I am well aware of the fact that the principal's entrance results in my becoming tense, yet the others don't seem to be as tense as I am. I simply suspect I am still in my "probationary period" and so I guess I find this matter particularly stressful.

At one elementary school we discovered that the principal's desk was placed inside the teachers' lounge. Teachers could pass by and see whether the principal was engaged in work or free to converse with them. The principal felt an integral part of the staff. In the same room, teachers reported an uneasy feeling due to the principal's presence there. The principal, however, was convinced that such an administrative structure was most favorable since it ensured maximal interaction between the principal and the teachers.

Aliza, a biology teacher in a general comprehensive school, was sitting in the teachers' lounge looking out of the window when to her surprise Uri, the principal, approached her and said:

> Aliza, I'd like to have a word with you. She wondered what he wanted and finally asked: "What did I do?" The principal replied: "Nothing, I just want to wish you a happy birthday." Aliza was pleased and asked

> him how he knew. Uri explained that Sharona, a member of the teachers' committee, notified him of such matters, and he made an effort to personally greet each teacher on his/her birthday. Although the event cheered Aliza, she also experienced a sense of confusion, since her first and instant response was like that of a guilty student.

In this particular teachers' lounge, there were times when we got the impression that with the principal's entrance, all the teachers turned into students and thus were regarded as being "a good class" or "a bad class." Israela, who has ten years of teaching experience at her present school, and another ten years in a former school, stated that the principal in her school entered the room when the bell rang and urged the teachers "to go to class." "Each time she does that I feel as confused as a vulnerable student." The principal in turn claims that

> These are good teachers; they only have bad habits. I certainly regard them as students simply because there is no other alternative. I am very strict on the matter of timing and I insist that teachers enter the class on time.

The relationships between teachers and a principal that are based on experiences in the lounge could have a positive influence on the nature of teachers' learning by sharing and communicating. On the other hand, the very presence of the principal in the lounge might transform a collaborative culture into one of contrived collegiality, thus diminishing the potential of the lounge as a productive site for teachers' professional development.

## Concluding Comments

The teachers' lounge constitutes a crossroads of interaction among adults in school. As we saw in the analysis presented above, principals might have various motives and reasons for entering the lounge, or for feeling alienated in it. Discrepancies of perceptions of leadership styles between principals and teachers on the one hand, and of the nature and function of the lounge on the other, might create problems of control and participation in schools. Clarification of these complex issues in teacher education (as described in chapter 9) and in practice could contribute to the improvement of the school climate. The lounges instantly reflect the set of relationships between teachers and principals in a school. Modes of interactions and their manifest expressions indicate whether there is an atmosphere of mutual understanding and support, or of antagonism and dislike.

Principals must keep this in mind and work to improve human relations in their schools and communities. Richardson, Short and Prickett (1993) claim that:

> Effective principles establish a climate in which the staff have a high level of satisfaction with their work. They also encourage a strong sense of participation and control over important educational decisions and activities in school. (p. 11)

A teacher's lounge, as Robbins & Alvy (1995) argue, is an area in schools used recently for developing opportunities for professional growth. Through institutionalizing professional interaction, reflection, and reading, the principal should be alert and ready to be involved in his teachers' professional development. They claim:

> Working to develop a professional lounge area in the school can be a significant professional boost for administrators and teachers. This should be an area to exchange professional articles, books, and ideas. Principals should encourage teachers to pass professional articles to the principal to help him or her stay on top of particular issues and, probably more important, remain informed regarding what teachers think is important.

> Having an area in the school for professional reading just might make it easier for administrators and teachers to spend time there during a school day . . . actually building the time into their weekly schedules. The actual physical structure for professional reflection can symbolize the importance of remaining on the cutting edge. (pp. 260–61)

The potential role of lounges as sites for professional development is treated in the next chapter.

# CHAPTER 8

# Professional Communities and Teacher Development

The development of professional communities of teachers has become one of the central concerns of educators and researchers. Several questions might be raised when dealing with the role of lounges in this context. What is the possible role of lounges in creating and sustaining professional communities? What features of lounges contribute to this role? This chapter deals with one of the major functions of the lounge, namely, providing an environment for teacher development.

## The Lounge as the Site for Development of Professional Communities

Let us start with the notion of professional community. Talbert & McLaughlin (1994) propose

> that professionalism among teachers is a product of social interaction and negotiation of norms within collegial work groups or networks. (p. 131)

We view such work groups or networks as teacher communities. The teachers' lounge might be seen as an ideal setting in which social interaction and negotiation of norms can take place, with the potential of leading to enhanced professionalism among teachers. Strong teaching communities evolving in lounges carry the promise of shared norms of practice and stronger teachers' professional commitments. The data of Talbert and McLaughlin reveal that

> teachers who participate in strong professional communities within their subject area departments or other teacher networks, have higher levels of professionalism, as measured in this study, than do teachers in less collegial settings. (ibid, pp. 142–43)

The prospects for enhancing professionalism are perceived by Talbert & McLaughlin (1994) to be determined locally as colleagues come to share standards for educational practice, including strong commitments to students and to their profession. In this view, local communities of teachers are the vehicles for enhanced professionalism in teaching (Talbert & McLaughlin, 1994, p. 145). And, according to Lieberman and Miller (1984),

> teachers must have opportunities to discuss, think about, try out and hone out new practices. (p. 93)

They suggest several ways of enabling teachers to do this in a school-based environment: one might create, for instance, new structures such as problem-solving groups or decision-making teams; or one might encourage a culture of inquiry as an ongoing part of teaching. The movement is toward

> long-term, continuous learning in the context of school and classroom and with the support of colleagues. (p. 596)

We believe that lounges, as a site for teachers' interactions, can provide the necessary conditions for the development of strong teacher networks, and would support the generation of shared knowledge about teaching. This knowledge could lead to more effective teaching.

The work of Rosenholtz (1989) concerning the workplace of teachers emphasizes the importance of teacher collaboration in ensuring the academic success of their students. She states that

> teachers' learning opportunities offer them a sense of ongoing challenge and continuous growth that makes greater mastery and control of their environment possible. (p. 7)

She argues, moreover, that teachers need fewer ego-endangering workplace circumstances in order to request and offer professional advice:

> Norms of collegiality enable if not compel teachers to request and offer advice and assistance in helping their colleagues improve. We also find that the greater teachers' opportunities for learning, the more their students tend to learn. (p. 7)

Our study describes the kinds of norms of collegiality developing in lounges that could provide the basis for teachers assisting one another. We perceive the lounge as an embodiment of suitable circumstances for the promotion of teacher collaboration and mutual learning, culminating in the creation of communal knowledge.

The interaction in the lounge is different from that between teachers in other environments, such as private homes. The context of the lounge is the context of immediate practice: the walls and tables bear the signs of professional activity, announcements of meetings, or stacks of tests. The limitation of time between the rings of the bell, as well as the concentration of many people within the limits of the lounge, do not allow for a sense of real leisure to develop. The intensity of the environment creates conditions for focusing on pressing professional matters, and for the growth of professional knowledge. This environment stimulates thinking and talking about matters in a highly concentrated form. The staff in their room are on transition time, between periods of teaching in classrooms. Any previous knowledge shared with others, or generated in the community of discourse, might be perceived as serving practice immediately. Shared communal professional knowledge is oriented toward the teaching of specific content areas, but it also relies heavily on the affective dimensions of teaching, such as caring for individual students, or the feelings of joy, sadness, or disenchantment that might accompany classroom teaching.

## Teachers' Collegiality

As discussed in chapter 2, teacher collegiality is deemed to be of utmost importance because it provides teachers with opportunities to acquire instructional range, depth, and flexibility (Little 1987). Interdependent collegiality has many advantages, sustaining an ongoing process of collaborative practices which might lead teachers to raise questions about their current practices, thus fostering pedagogical innovations (Grimmett & Crehan 1992). And yet this kind of collegiality is rare in schools. Hargreaves (1989) argues that the prevailing context of teachers' work is not compatible with interdependent collegiality, and one might find instead a culture of "contrived collegiality," which is characterized by

> a set of formal, specific bureaucratic procedures to increase the attention given to joint teacher planning and consultation. It can be seen in initiatives such as peer coaching, mentor teaching, joint planning in specially provided rooms, formally scheduled meetings and clear job descriptions, and training programs for these in consultative roles. (p. 9)

Hargreaves (1992) makes an interesting distinction between the "feminine" characteristics of collaborative cultures and the "masculine" style of contrived collegiality. According to Hargreaves, collaborative cultures are spontaneous, evolutionary, and unpredictable.

> They intermix the private and public, openly placing teachers' work in the context of their wider lives, biographies and purposes. (p. 235)

Contrived collegiality is viewed by Hargreaves as representing an imposed, regulated, and predictable mode, which superimposes the public sphere on the private, maintaining a separation between these two domains of teachers' lives.

Teachers' lounges do not belong in the category of contrived collegiality. Whatever happens there is not based on top-down initiatives. The lounge is a place where teachers enjoy private time in their own territory, a territory which represents the antithesis of contrived collegiality. Events in the lounge are usually unplanned, informal, and no bureaucratic regulations shape the ebb and flow of life in such rooms. As discussed in the chapter dealing with the blurring of boundaries, the lounge is an environment in which the borders between the private and public spheres of teachers' lives are blurred. It is this blurring which is conducive for the integration of the social and professional aspects of teachers' lives and is, therefore, conducive for the establishment of collaborative professional communities.

What are some of the features of collaborative professional communities can develop in the teachers' lounge without losing their capacity to join together the private and public spheres of their lives? One of the main elements is the development of knowledge-based communities of discourse.

## Communities of Discourse

Hornbrook (1989) claims that we are inescapably a part of communities of discourse, and that it is these communities of discourse that influence the way in which we think and speak. The communities of discourse which arise in teachers' lounges are involved in the creation of a special kind of knowledge. This special knowledge originates in the professional conversations that are held in the lounge and that are part of the teachers' everyday work. In the staffroom, the personal and practical knowledge of teachers, described and analyzed by Connelly & Clandinin (1988), is transformed into communal knowledge, through the process of interaction and sharing between members of the community of discourse. Connelly and Clandinin define personal practical knowledge as:

> A particular way of reconstructing the past and the intentions for the future to deal with the exigencies of a present situation. (p. 25)

They claim that one can use the term "personal practical knowledge" to emphasize the teacher's knowing of a classroom. We emphasize that this term can be borrowed to describe the teacher's knowing of their lounges as well, and can serve as a basis for communal knowledge.

The case of Shosh is one of the many examples in our study which illustrates sharing of teaching experiences and learning from each other. The discussion concerned alternative teaching strategies, such as group work. Through talking openly about the difficulties different teachers had encountered while trying group work in their classes, they were able to learn from each other about the complexities of organizing and sustaining this teaching mode.

The discourse in teachers' lounge may be interpreted as the pursuit of further knowledge. It is constructed of types of professional dialogue, along with types of socially intimate dialogue. Throughout this discourse a new type of knowledge is created: it is unique to teachers' lounges, and is not created in other contexts. We can define this type of knowledge as **communal knowledge**, referring to teacher's professional knowledge which is obtained through participating in events taking place within the lounge. Communal knowledge is based on the shared experience of the staff, and on the set of conventions established within the staffroom. The term "shared experiences" has a double meaning. First, teachers share their classroom experiences in the lounge and, second, the interactions in the lounge themselves constitute a set of shared experiences which could have far-reaching implications for the practice of these teachers, through the establishment of a common school ethos.

## Teachers as Learners

In his *Mind, Self and Society*, Mead (1934) has clarified that mankind creates a communicative process with the environment by means of stimulus and reaction, both of which use language. It is essential to understand the "role" that other participants play as well as one's own, in order to obtain a relationship based upon mutual understanding. To understand the communicative process in the lounge one has to be aware that the role a teacher chooses to play there might differ from the role adopted when entering the classroom.

In the teachers' lounge, teachers interact with adults, peers, and colleagues. The roles they choose to play help create the unwritten code of behavior that is practiced there. Such a many-layered behavioral text contains messages that can be deciphered by the participants. In their lounges, teachers might be conceived of as learners in a double sense. As inhabitants of the lounge they learn to comprehend its "text" and to be more knowledgeable about its functions and conventions. Thus, teachers might gain understanding of ways of acting and reacting in this environment. On the other hand, they learn to decipher the professional aspects of schooling as participants in the generation of communal knowledge in the lounge.

It is contended herewith that the special circumstances of behavior in teachers' lounges act as catalytic agents in the process of creating communal professional knowledge there. In that room, teachers behave simultaneously as teachers and learners. Through telling their stories and sharing their experiences they stimulate and support each other in constructing and shaping professional knowledge. Telling stories is one way of creating and sharing knowledge; this becomes part of the communal knowledge of their school and is at the basis of its ethos.

Corrie (1996) argues that, in the context of collegial collaboration,

> schools cannot afford to ignore the knowledge of talented individuals, even if it challenges established orthodoxy. Maintaining the school knowledge and excluding all other knowledge may carry a high price. (p. 246)

We must add as a cautionary note. There is a danger that the communal knowledge created in the school will tend to reflect the common denominator of existing traditional knowledge, and that the voices of innovative teachers will be overwhelmed. Our study leads us to view the lounge as a source of dynamic activity in which manifold voices interact. Thus, a balance is maintained between creating a communal school knowledge and maintaining individual expression. The interaction of manifold voices is clearly noticeable in the words of Naomi:

> The teachers' lounge is an important and vital place mainly because it allows teachers to argue, to express their opinions, to raise problems, and to search for solutions with one's colleagues. (Emphasis by the authors)

## Collective Remembering

Learning from experience is conceived as a socially constructed activity which may be understood in terms of collective remembering (Middleton & Edwards, 1990). Middleton and Edwards emphasize the theme of knowledge-sharing and using

> As a form of collective memory in work settings. (p. 16)

Orr (1990) analyzed the concept of community memory. According to Orr, the most characteristic feature of talk about work is its narrative structure. Orr states that

> The stories in the community memory are produced in the real work of diagnosis and are further useful because their form prepares them for use in the next narrative creation of sense out of facts. (p. 186)

Beyond the construction and sharing of knowledge, the narrative form of community memory fulfills another important function, the shaping of the professional identity of members of the community. The process of collective remembering is conceived here as crucial for the teaching profession, as teachers share their knowledge in the form of stories and narratives of events. Teachers' lounges can be an ideal setting for such collective remembering. Ben-Peretz (1995) claims that

> As one's individual professional identity is shaped through collective remembering, so does this process serve to establish the ethos of schools. Telling "our" stories and discussing their implications for action creates a common way of doing things in "our" school. The process of collective remembering becomes a channel for the induction of novice teachers to the culture of schools. (p. 140)

The shared professional knowledge of teachers determines how we evaluate students or how one deals with classroom management problems in our school. Structured communal knowledge is not static but highly dynamic, and it is reconstructed continuously because of the constant flow of information and the sharing of stories of experiences which characterize lounges.

As stated above, teachers learn, in the course of time, to be knowledgeable about the conventions and functions of their lounge. This is a part of professional knowledge that is generally not dealt with in pre- or in-service teacher education programs. And yet it constitutes an important component of knowledge about the context of teaching. We devote the next chapter to teacher education about lounges.

## Professional Development in the Lounge

McLaughlin (1994) declares that collaborative communities exist at different levels, such as departmental, school, district, or professional organization: there is an extent

> to which professional development is not a special project activity or only an in-service problem. Issues and opportunities for professional development occur in assorted forms, formats, and forums in the daily lives of teachers. (p. 47)

Her research indicates that

> Teachers singled out their professional discourse community as the reason that they have been successful in adapting to today's students, the source of their professional motivation and support, and the reason that they did not burn out in the face of some exceedingly demanding teaching situations. (p. 33)

McLaughlin emphasizes the importance of a common meeting area to provide the necessary environment for the development of professional collaborative communities. Our own study of teachers' lounges shows the room to be an ideal site for this purpose, since its function does not depend on external initiatives.

At this point, it is appropriate to mention three dimensions of teacher development which might be served by the collaborative communities. Bell & Gilbert (1994) view teacher development as containing the three following elements: the professional, the social, and the personal. *Professional development* is defined as the development of ideas and actions; *social development* refers to the development of collaborative ways of relating to other teachers; *personal development* concerns feelings. We shall provide examples of all these dimensions behind the lounge door, where events or interactions might serve the development of the above dimensions.

Although the process of generating communal knowledge is considered to be part of the culture of all teachers' lounges, its specific features might differ among various lounges and in diverse contexts of interaction among the staff. Teaching is often conceived as a profession without ranking and inner hierarchy. To paraphrase Gertrude Stein, "a teacher is a teacher is a teacher." Yet one can distinguish different groups of teachers in reference to their subject matter, their seniority, or their role in the school. The personal, practical, and professional knowledge of senior teachers, or department chairs, and their modes of knowing their educational situations (Connelly & Clandinin 1985) might be regarded by their colleagues in the lounge as more valuable than the personal knowledge of novice teachers. This kind of hierarchy is dependent on the environment of the lounges, and might be meaningless in other contexts. In a staff meeting held in a teacher's home, the special status of more senior teachers, or department chairs, might be much less important.

There are three categories of interpersonal relations in the teachers' lounges; they might have an impact on the creation of communal knowledge and professional development. Incidents in the lounge and the norms of participating teachers, as witnessed in our interviews and observations, serve to exemplify this point.

1. Interaction among peers.
2. Interaction between novice and veteran teachers.
3. Interaction between teachers and principal. This type of relationship was treated in chapter 7.

### *1. Interaction among Peers*

During breaks in the teachers' lounge, Debby sits close to the table of the English teachers, "where they regularly exchange comments over what is happening in their classes, what has succeeded or failed. Instructional material is exchanged along with the coffee." Debby confessed that sitting there gives her a sense of belonging, a place where her feelings of joy or despair can be expressed freely. She states: "My best friends sit here, and they understand me best." In Debby's staffroom, during the breaks, teachers usually sit in the company of colleagues who teach the same subject, creating a regular pattern. She claims that this is only natural since teaching has always been divided into subjects. She regards this division as most appropriate. "It's true that a teachers' lounge can lead to meeting all kinds of teachers; however, it's better to sit by a 'regular' table and feel 'at home'." This was the picture drawn by Debby in her interview. Debby has ten years of teaching experience, six of which she spent at the same high school. Close and daily interactions among those who teach the same subject provide ample opportunities for professional and social development.

In another high school, in the teachers' lounge, political debates are a daily occurrence, perhaps due to the location of the place near the border, or due to the high political awareness of its population. The way in which the chairs are arranged is not fixed, is not immovable. The teachers form ad hoc groups based on the subjects being discussed. Miriam claims:

> The teachers' lounge is crowded, disgusting, and totally unaesthetic, yet a magic wand draws me in to participate in the discussions taking place there. Relationships that form within the teachers' lounge eventually grow into friendships beyond the daily work encounters.

In this manner, the rooms may be perceived as fostering the social development of the staff, the ability to relate to other teachers.

These examples indicate that teachers' lounges adopt their own mode of discourse. The specific style of interactions is derived without any interference from a higher authority but as a direct outcome of conventions and forms of discourse. These forms of discourse create a subculture which is molded by the teachers, and which provides the basis for forming a collaborative culture.

Naomi, as mentioned above, describes this process:

> The teachers' lounge is an important and vital place mainly because it allows teachers to argue, to express their opinions, to raise problems, and to search for solutions with one's colleagues.
>
> This enables teachers to change their views, or their teaching strategies following the discussion there, when one finds out that the previous strategies may not be appropriate for one's students.

This quote describes vividly how teachers develop professional ideas and actions. The lounge is perceived as a site for professional encounters. The discourse which develops there helps teachers solve problems in their practice. The immediacy of these professional interactions in the physical context of teaching gives them the power to increase their own awareness, their own ways of knowing educational situations.

*2. Interaction between Novices and Senior Teachers*

New teachers, i.e., those who have only recently become a part of the school staff, have to adapt to the existing subcultures; only after doing this will they feel "at home" in the lounge. New teachers have to cope with the stress of new demands and have to prove themselves professionally. One of their first tasks is usually to communicate with the senior teachers in the school, to win their trust, and possibly friendship. Bearing in mind that each staff maintains its own norms in the context of subject matter subcultures within the teachers' lounge, the new teacher soon realizes that it is necessary to get acquainted with the process we defined as the creation of communal knowledge. The new teacher, attempting to minimize the inevitable gap between former learning and the learning going on in the lounge, might be very hesitant. Overcoming these gaps is part of a teacher's induction into practice through his/her participation in the community of discourse in the teachers' lounge, among colleagues. This is a process by which the new teacher's future competence might be determined. Yet this process is not an easy one and could sometimes be hampered by the nature of interactions in the lounge, especially if accompanied by mutual misunderstandings.

Young teachers tend to feel like outsiders; Ronnie, a teacher in his first year comments:

> I'm uncomfortable and feel that I'm being judged all the time. Perhaps it's a matter of seniority and in the course of time I will get used to it.

Lisa recalls the bad feeling that had accompanied her first months of teaching:

> Senior teachers are, as a rule, snobbish. When at last they do inquire whether you are getting along, they don't even bother to listen to the answer.

Jane, another teacher who looks particularly young, aggressively declares that

> Senior teachers tend to pressurize me. They don't create a pleasant atmosphere. They simply don't assist or anticipate. They're always "inspecting" you and your appearance. Everyday someone remarks that I look like a teenager myself. In fact, I wouldn't mind if a few of the teachers retired early.

When novice teachers are confronted with veteran teachers, a problem of status tends to arise. Let us refer to Adam who, in his first year of teaching, states:

> The mentality which governs the teachers' lounge disgusts me. There are miserable female teachers who, I suspect, are in need of psychological help, as

> well as cosmetic care. However, most of the male teachers are no better. I feel very frustrated, surrounded by this atmosphere into which I'm slowly sinking and which does not reflect well on any of the senior teachers.

Adam differentiates between male teachers and female teachers, yet he also refers to the seniors as a monolithic group that reflects defeat. He sees ugliness around him and feels repelled, which makes it extremely difficult for him to become part of their community of discourse.

> I would like to make them laugh, to inquire what was so tragic, yet I am afraid they would consider me a "nuisance."

At first Adam tried to establish contact with a number of the senior teachers by informing them about his work in class. He had expected encouragement but the general response was: "Never mind, it will be easier in the days to come," or "I've been through it myself." Adam had started his working life motivated by concepts of innovation and change, and an autonomous perception of teaching. However, when confronted with the indifference of some senior teachers, he sensed they had constructed a solid wall around themselves which was growing higher and which was seen by him as dangerous to his own professional well-being.

Adam faces a dilemma: should he extend his efforts to establish contact with the senior staff, or should he break off from them? Most new teachers are anxious for some special care and personal relations, rather in the way that a new student in class struggles to determine his/her status within the group. Integration within the teachers' lounge has a great effect on the young teacher's decision as to whether he/she will remain a teacher. An example of this can be seen in the case of a literature teacher, who admitted she had quit teaching at one school because of the staffroom, which she regarded as a "hornet's nest." She found her colleagues there troublesome, contemptible, and all too happy to gossip. In contrast to these descriptions, there exist reports describing support and assistance. Some teachers' lounges have a round table in the center. In those rooms, even if there are predefined groups, the atmosphere is one of acceptance and cooperation. In such circumstances there are manifold opportunities for a teacher's personal and social development. The physical and social environments which characterize different lounges determine the possibilities of collaboration and sharing, which, in turn, lead to forms of communal knowledge.

Yet the general picture clearly indicates that there is a distinction between new and veteran teachers. Naomi, who teaches at a high school, confessed during her interview that

> most of the senior teachers are very old. There exists a sense of reverence towards them, partly due to the fact that they are a strongly consolidated group whose code of language is exclusive to them. Thus only a few of us younger teachers have succeeded in interacting with them.

A possible explanation for the experiences of these new teachers is based on the notion of the origination of communal knowledge in the lounge. This knowledge has usually grown over many years: it might be expressed in "code words" and it is extremely difficult for newcomers to interpret it or to join in its ongoing development. Moreover, such knowledge cannot be acquired passively: it has to be constructed through active engagement in the discourse, and novice teachers might be shut out or might act only on the fringe of this process.

This interpretation is reinforced from the opposite point of view. Noga, a senior teacher admits that

> They are too young and I feel like "the old billy-goat." With my experience, what can a younger teacher possibly offer me? Thus cooperation between us can

> be made possible only on the basis of ourselves acting as mentors.

Thus the novice teacher is effectively made to stay outside the community of discourse among equals.

In the teachers' lounge, we are apt to find complex encounters, imbued with problems between two different biological and professional generations, each of whom criticizes the other, tests the other. Whether it is deliberate or not, many senior teachers create an invisible wall to protect their privacy; breaking through this barrier is enormously difficult for novice teachers. Yet the interaction between the older and the younger teachers is essential if the process of mutual learning—learning from one another—is to take place.

## Concluding Comments

Recent approaches to schooling emphasize the role of teachers as learners as well as the positive impact of professional communities in schools on the improvement of practice. In this chapter we suggest that teachers' lounges are optimal sites for the creation of such communities and provide, by their very nature, opportunities for teacher development in the personal, social, and professional dimensions. Through social interaction, the sharing of experiences, and a collective recollection of school events, teachers develop communal knowledge about teaching.

Clandinin & Connelly (1995) discuss the different ways in which teachers know their practice. They talk about the "secret stories" that teachers tell each other concerning their professional experiences. Those stories are filled with graphic details of everyday life in class, strongly flavored with emotions. On the other hand, policymakers, curriculum developers, and researchers create sacred stories about ways of knowing education and educational action, which are perceived by teachers as prescriptive and morally obligatory.

According to Clandinin & Connelly (1986), these two kinds of stories might be in conflict, causing uneasiness and confrontation for teachers. We agree that teachers' lounges can serve as natural meeting places between secret and sacred stories. The communal knowledge emanating in the lounge has the potential to be based on an organic link between the private and personal knowledge of individual teachers and the policies, directives, curricula, and research findings that are imposed on them from outside.

This localized, contextualized communal knowledge can be formed only through face-to-face interactions between teachers. Teachers have the need and the will to share their stories with each other and to know more about the ways in which the "other" conducts his/her lessons. The lounge provides an appropriate site for such interactions.

CHAPTER 9

# Implications for Teacher Education

A recurring question about research in education is concerned with its possible implications for the practice of schooling and teaching. We address this question through a discussion of some of the implications of our study of teachers' lounges for the process of teacher education. The main point of this book concerns the existence of a number of physical and cultural territories in schools which constitute a complex web of interdependence. Teacher education programs which do not reflect this complexity fail to provide students-teachers with a valid view of their future professional lives.

The main focus of teacher education programs lies on the preparation of teachers for classroom practice. This is, obviously, an issue of major importance and yet it is claimed herewith that extending the study of schooling to include other territories, such as teachers' lounges, would provide insights into additional aspects of the teaching profession, and would therefore be helpful for introducing students-teachers to their workplace.

We will start our discussion with some general comments on the social background of teacher education on one hand, and on the gendered nature of this profession, on the other. It could be argued that a lounge which provides strong and helpful support for teachers might counteract some of the societal forces and prejudices that tend to control teacher education. Yet the prerequisite for this influence is that the issues be discussed openly in pre- and in-service teacher education programs.

Feiman-Nemser & Floden (1986) argue that

> Teachers not only work in classrooms, they also work in institutions which surround them with constraints and opportunities. These organizational properties represent a second source of influence on the cultures of teaching. Finally, schools function in a larger social context that shapes and is, in turn, shaped by what goes on there. Thus the cultures of teaching also reflect the influence of economic, social, and political factors. (p. 515)

It is our thesis that, to a certain extent, the teacher's lounge represents the constraints and opportunities of schools as institutions, as shown in some of the events described earlier. Learning about life in the staffroom as well as the forces at work in this context should be considered important elements of teacher education. We feel that it is necessary that student-teachers be made aware of those aspects of teaching so that they will be able to and to understand some—if not all—of the intricacies inherent in their professional environment.

## Societal Forces

Britzman (1986) argues that the prevalent processes of teacher education reinforce the status quo and tend to sustain the social structure of schooling. She claims that

> Teaching is fundamentally a social relationship, characterized by mutual dependency, social interaction, and social engagement. Individualizing the social basis of teaching dissolves the social context, establishing instead the supposed autonomy and very real isolation of the teacher in the current

> school structure. Once the student teacher is severed from the social context of teaching, the tendency is to reproduce rather than to challenge her or his institutional biography. The values embedded in the institutional biography become sedimented, and serve as the foundation for the cultural myths which legitimize a hierarchical image of authority, a reified view of knowledge and a rugged individualist stance. (p. 453)

According to Britzman, one outcome of the individualization of learning to teach is the reproduction of school structure. We find an echo of this orientation in Gordon's (1996) approach. Gordon claims that teacher development leading to the transformation of schools is a collective process, occurring in the context of a specific school ethos. Pre-service teacher education, on the other hand, focuses on the individual acquiring basic professional knowledge and does not, usually, prepare teachers for the kind of interactions which foster the development of communal engagement in educational change. We believe that it is important to create professional community experiences for teachers in the pre-service stages of their development in order to start the process of shared development.

A staffroom which houses a vital and powerful teaching community could act as an antidote against the denial of the social basis of teaching. Instead of legitimizing a hierarchical image of authority and an individualistic stance, the complete involvement of teachers in the social interaction and mutual dependency of lounges would allow questions to be raised about the status quo, and would encourage the possibility of introducing changes. Yet, such processes have to become part of teacher education programs, so that future teachers will acknowledge the fact that peer relationships, as well as life in staffrooms, are a central component of the teaching profession. This approach to teacher socialization is in line with changes in the view of teachers as lonely and professionally isolated, as discussed above. The notion of teachers as learners in professional communities relates to an important issue in teacher education, namely, the cultivation of autonomous and independent teachers while simultaneously strengthening their dispositions and abilities to collaborate with their colleagues.

## Gender Issues

One critical issue of the social reality of schooling concerns the issue of gender. Most teachers are women, and this numerical domination has led to a prevailing view of teaching as women's work. It has also affected the status of teaching. Feiman-Nemser & Floden (1986) claim that

> Feminism has contributed to rising expectations for women, but the social image of teachers has remained the same or perhaps has even diminished. Once the job for ordinary men, teaching is now seen as ordinary work for ordinary women. (p. 519)

The question is: how might this state of affairs influence processes of change within schools?

Teachers appear to make relatively little effort to initiate and implement antisexist activities. Acker (1988) argues that, among other causes, the conditions of teachers' work may not be conducive to such innovations. She discusses several factors which might determine the feasibility of teachers' involvement in promoting antisexist reforms. Teachers' adhesion to the classroom base and their commitment to ensuring classroom order and regular practice, are considered to be factors that counteract the possibility to work for change. Another factor concerns teacher isolation and the lack of opportunities for cooperation with colleagues. Acker states that not only is teacher culture thought to emphasize autonomy, but

> the geography of the school sometimes imposes it. (p. 317)

Here again we see a crucial role for teachers' lounges to create environments for cooperation and collaboration among the staff. The "geography" of the school changes when the lounge becomes a center for teachers' activities outside their classrooms.

Another facet of the social aspect of teaching concerns the **micropolitics of schools**, which also contribute to the apparent passivity of teachers. Ball (1987) views schools as organizations in which individuals compete in order to serve their own interests and satisfactions. In a competitive situation which is characterized by conflict it is difficult to collaborate to bring about innovations. In our study we called one of the factors the "political factor," which expresses competition and conflict. This appears to be a natural component of life in schools, and is reflected in the lounge. We have seen, though, that this is not a dominant component in the perception of most teachers, and that some of the events that take place in the lounge might be understood to have the opposite effect through a cathartic process.

Gender issues play a role in the power structure of schools, with women having a relatively powerless position, especially vis-à-vis male principals (Ben-Peretz 1996; Casey & Apple 1984). Teacher narratives provide insights into aspects of teaching as seen from a gender point of view. For instance, a retired elementary school teacher, recalling her previous experiences of teaching new immigrant students, says:

> It was extremely difficult for me. On top of that the principal had very specific demands. He used to come into my class to evaluate the use of the blackboard. The school climate was competitive instead of cooperative. Maybe because of the principal's manner it turned out to be a case of "each person for herself." (Ben-Peretz, p. 181)

The principal described in the above paragraph created a competitive climate in his school and managed to undermine the professional confidence of the narrator through his constant supervision and the withdrawal of her instructional autonomy. This story exemplifies the potential for antagonism between female teachers and male administrators in schools as mentioned by Casey & Apple (1984), and the kind of social control of teachers in such gendered situations. It is our claim that teachers' lounges might counteract such tendencies. The interactions among teachers, which are not imposed by school authorities, might be viewed as a source for empowerment, providing opportunities for overcoming some of the difficulties that teachers experience in the micropolitics of the power relationships of their profession.

Student-teachers would benefit from a careful introduction into these issues. The following paragraphs present ways of dealing with the initiation of student-teachers into the complexities of peer relations in school.

## Initiation into the Culture of Teachers' Lounges

The past experiences of student-teachers in schools, as former students, might be conceived as playing a crucial role in their learning to be teachers (Lortie 1975). Student-teachers come to teacher education programs with an extended experience as former students. They usually remember well the norms and conventions governing life in classrooms. Yet, student-teachers do not have memories of the inside culture of teachers' lounges; for them the lounge used to be forbidden territory. What happened behind the closed doors of the teachers' lounge was a secret for students, a secret that sometimes raised their curiosity. Examples of this curiosity are presented in some of the monologues. Future teachers could benefit greatly from gaining some insights into this foreign culture, the culture of teachers' room. Such insights could make their induction period teaching more productive and rewarding, and would enable newly qualified teachers to become more easily a part of the community of teachers in school. It was argued above that teachers are learners in the lounge, learning simultaneously about the social environment in the lounge, and about their profession. Without some prior knowledge and experience concerning lounges, newcomers to the profession might make unfortunate mistakes in their attempts to become full members in the community of teachers, and their induction period might be extremely painful. As discussed above, we view strong teaching communities in schools as the basis for teacher development and for school change and improvement.

## Features of Lounges and their Meaning for Teacher Education

Several features of lounges emerging from our analysis of lounges are considered to be pertinent for teacher education. These are as follows: the lounge as a learning environment, the nature of collegiality among teachers, the cathartic process in the lounge, social cohesion, and the interactions between the teachers and their principals in the staffroom.

The **learning environment** provided by lounges is one of the facets of the culture of teaching which could and should be treated in teacher education programs. Communal knowledge generated in interactive processes among professionals could be included as part of the knowledge base of teaching. Student-teachers could experience the learning environment of a staffroom from the perspective of its contribution to professional growth.

Another important issue concerns the **nature of collegiality** among teachers, the norms of collegiality and the perceptions of a "good colleague" that constitute part of the ethos of schools. Student-teachers might have numerous opportunities to reflect on the meaning of being a "good teacher." Such reflections usually focus on matters of classroom interactions and modes of instruction. Yet teachers are also participants in a complex web of interpersonal relations with their peers, their principal, and other adults who are part of the school community. A major part of these relationships take place in the teachers' lounge. Awareness of the existence of norms of collegiality, and the ability to interpret their significance, might be crucial for teachers, especially for the newly qualified ones who are strangers to the web of interpersonal relations among the staff. As described above, a new teacher might occupy a certain seat in the lounge and feel the "hostility" that this action creates around her. She might feel worried and embarrassed despite her being unaware of the norms of the allocation of seats in this specific lounge.

Several processes, acceptable within the walls of the staffroom, might be misinterpreted by student teachers and newly qualified ones and thus give rise to confusion and conflict. The **cathartic process** in the teachers' room, might be misunderstood as simple grumblings and complaints, and might be seen as

> narrations of difficulties that nobody intends to change. (Keinan, 1994, p. 115)

Student-teachers who share this view might be reluctant to participate in the process, missing the opportunity it provides for relieving feelings of anger, frustration, and fear, and for paving the way for finding a solution to the many problems involved in teaching.

**Social cohesion** in the lounge (the *Gibush* phenomenon) is one of its major features. Student teachers and novice teachers who feel they are outsiders in the lounge might benefit from being introduced to this aspect of teaching while still in their pre-service program. It might be as important for teachers to be considered good colleagues by their peers, as it is for them to be considered good teachers in their classrooms. By learning to work and study together, student-teachers will be prepared for the kind of interaction which fosters the development of communal engagement in educational change.

A common feature of lounges concerns the **interactions between teachers and the principal** whenever he or she enters the lounge (Schonmann & Ben-Peretz 1993). An experienced teacher who had worked for three different principals maintained:

> The entrance of principals into the lounge creates stress and it is difficult to understand why this is so.

We described one elementary school where the principal used to work in the teachers' lounge; the teachers reported that they felt uneasy about the regular presence of the principal in their lounge, whereas the principal thought that her presence eased communication with the teachers.

The discrepancy between the way in which principals and teachers perceive their relationships in the lounge is a common phenomenon and deserves to be dealt with in teacher education programs as part of the culture of schools. The nature of interactions between principals and teachers merits attention in the process of professionalization of principals. A literature of cases concerning these interactions could prove useful to teachers, as well as to principals. Of special interest are case studies of principals whose work has taken them into different kinds of staffrooms. Such studies would provide insights into the links between different territories in schools and might offer opportunities for fruitful reflection on the complexities of school cultures.

## Some Suggestions for Including Teachers' Lounges in the Curriculum of Teacher Education

A good starting-point would be to include **guided observations of teachers' lounges** in the practicum. Student-teachers could be asked to describe the ecological characteristics of various lounges, using videotapes, photographs, drawings, and even three-dimensional models in their descriptions. These descriptions and visualizations would provide ample data for discussing the relationship between the structure and function of lounges. **Student-teachers might interview experienced teachers** about their lounges and try to understand various aspects of this apparently simple but, in reality, highly complex site and its potential impact on the culture of schools. Student-teachers could write **journals** about their own experience in the lounge during their teaching practice, and gain better insights into the nature of peer relationships between adults in schools. Conducting mini-studies of life in lounges is another way of introducing student-teachers to professional and personal relationships among adults in schools.

**Role playing techniques** can be devised which would enable student-teachers to act out the various roles, conventions, dilemmas, and conflicts which characterize teachers' lounges. These games could include meetings with parents and/or students in the lounge, as well as visits from the principal. Notions of norms of collegiality, catharsis, and other aspects of the lounge would become alive in such situations. Student-teachers are usually involved in planning lessons and teaching units; teacher education programs could also demand the planning of teachers' activities in the lounge. Through this process the student-teacher becomes a partner in the creation of communal knowledge through different kinds of discourse.

Finally, it would be advisable to set up a **lounge for student-teachers in the teacher education institution** which would be a natural environment for the creation of a professional community, engaged in learning and professional growth. Habits of collaboration formed in such a lounge could be transferred to the future "real" places of work. Since student-teachers are engaged in their training, there exists a real need for them to share and discuss their experiences in a natural setting of their own without supervision and external guidance. Student-teachers, like their experienced colleagues, need a safe haven where they can speak freely about their concerns, their triumphs, and their tribulations. A lounge for student-teachers could be the ideal environment for professional reflection, for sharing experiences and opinions, for supporting each other, and for cathartic experiences. In their own lounge, the students might generate innovative ideas, and try to plan new solutions to old and new problems in education. They might even come up with unprecedented ways of conceptualizing and organizing the lounge itself in the institute of teacher education.

Students who experience their own lounge, and learn about the norms and conventions in lounges, and then enter schools as novice teachers, might not feel they are "outsiders" in this environment, and might move more smoothly into their new role as members of the community of teachers.

## Concluding Comments

We have outlined a framework for introducing and analyzing experiences in lounges, as an integral component of teacher education programs. Because of the strong social elements characterizing lounges, the experiences provide opportunities for raising questions about the status quo, and for dealing with issues of equity and justice, gender, and the power structure of schools. In the pre-service phase, the goals of student-teachers are usually oriented more toward survival in classrooms, but we claim that survival and engagement in teachers' lounges should complement this process. It is a missing link in teacher education.

Learning about staffrooms and their functions may provide student-teachers with an opportunity to get acquainted with issues mentioned in previous chapters, such as norms of collegiality, as well as possible connections between life in the lounge and student achievement in school. Lampert & Loewenberg-Ball (1998) argue that teacher education is better understood

> as a process of being inducted into a community of practice with its own tools, resources, shared ideas and debates. (p. 37)

Inducting student-teachers into the role of teacher lounges serves this process.

# Epilogue: Paradoxes in the Lounge

Having gained new understandings about teacher's life in lounges, we found that it is a place in which many opposites coexist—turbulence and noise versus quiet and tranquillity; rest versus work; public versus private; a race for student achievement versus the social function; external constraints versus independent activities.

It is our claim that these paradoxes might be at the root of much of the involvement of teachers in their lounges. We shall present these paradoxes as a common thread that weaves through the various aspects of lounges as presented in this book.

## Turbulence and Noise versus Quiet and Calmness

Teachers tend to perceive their lounges as crowded, noisy, and busy places but, paradoxically, the lounge is also perceived as a sanctuary of rest and tranquillity. The beehive metaphor expresses the turbulence, whereas the home metaphor portrays tranquillity. At different times, for different people, one or the other of these features is more predominant and colors their perception of the lounge but, basically, lounges are both noisy and quiet, turbulent and calm. This inherent paradox might account for the attracting-repelling power of lounges on their inhabitants, as indicated in their monologues. This ambiguity might be conceived as playing a role in teachers' burnout, and as an important component in the induction of novice teachers.

## Rest and Relaxation versus Work and Engagement in Accountable Activities

The paradox of these contradictory characteristics lies in the apparent change in the perception of work. It is puzzling that work conducted in the lounge, such as the grading of tests, the preparation of lesson plans, or collaboration with colleagues, does not seem to diminish the sense of rest experienced by teachers in their lounges.

The root metaphor of the kitchen that is used by teachers to describe their lounge encompasses both sides of this paradox. Kitchens suggest a feeling of warmth and belonging, as well as a feeling of being engaged in the basic processes of providing food. In the classroom context, teachers have to be in a state of constant awareness of the situation, ready to intervene at a moment's notice. Lounges provide a more relaxed nonthreatening environment in which even work is perceived as part of leisure. One of the reasons accounting for this phenomenon might be the fact that, in the lounge, teachers are surrounded by their colleagues, peers, and equals. The entrance of the principal changes this equilibrium; a teacher grading tests when the principal enters the lounge might feel under supervision and at "work."

## The Lounge as a Public as well as Private Place

The blurring of boundaries is a characteristic feature of teachers' lounges. This blurring creates the paradox of a site which, though public, allows individuals to sense liberation from the pressure of the constant surveillance of others, a pressure that accompanies their lives in public. In spite of the fact, and to a certain extent, because teachers are in an atmosphere of togetherness in the lounge, they have the opportunity to be on their own, as individuals who enjoy private time on the backstage of their professional existence. In classrooms they are "the teacher," a being whose individual traits are usually masked by the common features of teaching, which tend to be very powerful. Among peers and friends, they can become themselves and sometimes express this feeling very clearly. Becoming themselves creates another a paradoxical situation in which the "real selves" of teachers confront their peers, leading either to a sense of belonging to the community and identifying with it or, conversely, to a sense of loneliness and alienation. Thus, the myth of the lonely teacher is not confined to loneliness in the classroom, but might reappear in certain situations as loneliness in the lounge.

Several professional and social regularities in the lounge were identified in our study, such as joint planning and sharing of experiences, as well as drinking coffee and gossiping. These regularities take place in a context which is inherently in constant flux and a state of transition. The lounge is simultaneously an open and a closed space, and is characterized by a blurring of boundaries.

## The Social Function of the Lounge and its Link to Student Achievement

Teachers who are members of a socially vital community tend to work better together in the creation of communal knowledge, and in the development of a more successful practice. This relationship has been demonstrated in chapter 6 which analyzes the connection between experiences in the lounge and students' achievements. Teachers in high-achievement schools perceive the characteristics of the social function as a more appropriate description of their lounge than those in low-achievement schools. This link between the social function of lounges and student achievement is paradoxical, since one might expect teachers in high-achieving schools to view the work function as the most appropriate description of their lounge.

## Autonomy versus External Constraints

In the midst of the freedom and autonomous activities of teachers in the lounge, one might find intense, intentional, and focused involvement in the affairs of the school. Teachers are simultaneously free and constrained in their lounges. Their freedom is to a certain extent imaginary and their activities are determined by the demands and priorities of the school. We suggest that the specific context of the lounge, which is situated in the school building, determines this interplay of freedom and constraints. In their lounges teachers are simultaneously inside and outside the throb of school life, moving from one framework to the other. It might well be that, in the lounge, one framework reinforces and strengthens the other.

## Elaborating the Notion of Paradoxes

We found that the complex nature of the lounge does not prevent teachers from constructing a professional communal knowledge about teaching, nor does it prevent them from understanding the culture of their schools. The growth of teachers' professional behavior is increased and enriched by these complexities. The many stories in this book show that teachers hold and use their knowledge in distinctive ways which enable them to transform knowledge from the stage of the personal and practical to that of the communal and practical. Through the various modes of inquiry we used in this book we became aware of the fact that the paradoxes characterizing the lounges are intrinsic to teacher's lives there. We came to realize that these paradoxes enable us to develop an understanding of the world of adults/teachers in schools, and to see more clearly their social acts and the professional deeds.

The teachers' lounge is the primary site for developing interpersonal relationships among teachers, as well as between teachers and principals. It is a place where teachers gather and where they have manifold opportunities to express their common professional and social interests. Joy and pride, as well as sadness and despair, are revealed in teachers' interactions. Conflict situations involving students, colleagues, and superiors are played out in the lounge, and can lead to harmonious solutions or to disruptive strife. Hidden beyond these situations one is able to discern the inherent paradoxes in the culture of teachers' lounges mentioned above.

We view the teachers' lounge as constituting a dialectic of situations. Every facet of life in the lounge contains its opposite, creating a vital, complex, changing, and ever-surprising niche in the culture of schools. We believe this calls for further study and exploration.

In his book *The Kind of Schools We Need,* Eisner (1998) argued: "The only way I know to discover the salient and significant features of schools is to look. The implications of what is found will depend on what is found and on the educational values that give direction to the schools themselves" (p. 168). Eisner claimed that to look at schools is not enough, "The trick is to see" (p. 168). Thus to see what happens in lounges requires not only a willingness and sensibility to look at what is occurring there, but also requires that we use modes of inquiry that enable us to point to distinctive features of the life that teachers lead in their lounges. We must be able to discern the possibilities of this life, as well as the built-in constraints, which can discourage change, such as building the kinds of schools we need.

Looking carefully at teachers' lounges, attempting to see beyond the surface of everyday situations, we identified the five paradoxes mentioned above. These paradoxes form a substantial structure (Schwab 1964) built upon two clusters of parameters. One cluster is seen by us as pertaining to the individual, the person, and his or her needs and aspirations. This cluster includes the following parameters of lounges: quiet and calmness; rest and relaxation; privacy; the social function; autonomy.

The second cluster is seen by us as pertaining to the milieu, its conditions, and the context of words. This cluster includes the following parameters of lounges: noise; work and engagement in accountable activities; public place; student achievement; external constraints.

We picture this substantial structure as reflecting the tension between the individual and the environment inherent in the reality of lounges. The dynamic relationships evolving in the lounge as reflected in the paradoxes might be conflicting or synergetic, but they usually find their expression in a blurring of boundaries between the various parameters.

Our research showed that lounges are dynamic, complex, and intense environments, despite their appearance of simplicity and transparency. The substantive structure leads to sets of further research questions concerning life in these rooms. We suggest a scheme for generating research questions. This scheme is a two-dimensional chart in which the different parameters of the clusters of paradoxes constitute two poles as shown in the following:

| | quiet | rest | privacy | social function | autonomy |
|---|---|---|---|---|---|
| noise | | | | | |
| work | | | | | |
| public space | | | | | |
| student achievement | | | | | |
| external constraints | | | | | |

The cells in the chart depict the interactions of variables and could serve as starting points for further study. For instance, the interaction between autonomy of teachers and the work parameter might give rise to questions concerning the relationship between different modes of teacher collaboration in the lounge and teacher autonomy. The possible interactions between teachers' privacy and the external constraints imposed in the lounge might stimulate questions such as how teachers cope with regulations and norms of acting in lounges, and how these constraints interfere with their privacy.

Through the use of the chart, one may uncover the nature of conflicts or the potential synergetic effects, that arise from the complexity of the paradoxes which characterize the nature of the teachers' lounge.

We started our voyage through the territory of teachers' lounges by attempting to familiarize ourselves with their landscapes, and to raise the awareness of educators to the importance of deciphering the inner grammar of interactions in the lounge. Closing our book by highlighting the inherent paradoxes of life in lounges, and the new questions evolving from this framework, aims at expanding our understanding of teachers' development and the creation of professional communities in schools. We believe that educational practice might also benefit through developing ideas for teacher education programs and for the organization of schools, leading to the growth of functional communities of teachers.

# Appendix I

## Location and Interior Design of Teachers' Lounges in Israel

The following is a description of the location and interior design of some teachers' lounges in Israel.

Various studies and different planning perceptions of school buildings tend to agree that the teachers' lounge, whether it serves as a place for rest or for work, or for both of these functions, should be located within the administrative part of the school building. The administration largely determines the events taking place in school. It generally consists of the principal's office, and rooms for other officeholders, such as the vice-principal, department chairs, curriculum consultants, as well as the teachers' lounge. According to Blass & Avram (1988), it is customary that 6 to 8 percent of the net grounds of all buildings are assigned to administration. They argue that the allocation of administrative functions in school is based mainly upon two central factors: (a) the organizational or managerial structure, that is to say, the division into suborganizational units, and (b) the managerial style, whether centralized or decentralized. The more centralized the school management type is, the more the administrative functions will be located in the main administration area. Conversely, in a school with a decentralized management style, the functions of the administration and other officeholders are physically located near the subunits they are related to, serving their requirements.

What implications does this have for the site of the teachers' lounge? In schools with one administration, one large room is usually assigned to the lounge, to be shared by all teachers.

When the school administration is divided into subsections and subunits, it is natural that there will be at least two teachers' lounges, or even a number of teachers' lounges of different types and sizes, located in different sections of the buildings. Consequently a dilemma arises concerning the location of the teachers' lounge. On one hand, there is a desire to unify the teachers' staff as a whole without any distinction between different units, resulting in the establishment of only one teachers' lounge for the whole school. On the other hand, the concentration of many teachers in one room, however large, causes problems of overload, density, noise, and other microclimatic concerns that result in restricting the functioning of the lounge. In such conditions, Blass & Avram (1988) suggest the possibility of dividing the area assigned to the teachers' lounge into two or three rooms of different sizes. Each room would be capable of containing specific activities, and teachers could choose where to go. It is possible that during a short break teachers would prefer to stay in the larger lounge, where they could meet more colleagues. During a free period, however, teachers might prefer a smaller room in order to work, read, and be engaged in various individual activities.

According to the common concept of planning school buildings, it is desirable to locate the administration close to the school entrance, since guests and visitors who arrive at the school usually need to reach these offices. It is the custom that all administration offices be located as close as possible to the school entrance, so "strangers" do not have a chance to roam around unsupervised. The very location of the administration offices in a central point near the school entrance also enables the staff to supervise all events taking place in the school building and school yard.

In principle, the teachers' lounge ought to be located near the school administration department for the following functional reasons: The teachers require various secretarial services. The proximity of the teachers' lounge to the other administration offices contributes to the continuous daily interaction between the teachers and the principal.

Whatever the circumstances, it is necessary to remember that privacy, intimacy, and quiet are essential requirements for teachers' lounges; the interior design of these rooms is therefore an important factor in shaping the physical reality of these centers for the day-to-day working life of teachers.

## The Interior Design of the Teachers' Lounge

Three aspects of interior planning will be considered in this section, as described in Rubin, Avram, and Avner (1984): the aesthetic, the microclimatic and the functional.

**The Aesthetic Aspect:** This aspect is reflected in the choice of colors and materials. The colors of each and every item in the lounge, the type of finish, the shade of the walls and windows, and the density of objects present in the teachers' lounge, all contribute to the aesthetic aspect. Viewing the interior elements of the lounge in terms of aesthetics and, in particular, the maintenance of harmony between the various items, contributes a great deal to the creation of a pleasant environment.

**The Microclimatic Aspect:** The desirable microclimatic environment concerns the supply of required natural/artificial lighting; suitable ventilation, so that the temperature will be comfortable in both summer and winter; and the lack of acoustic or visual disturbances. The careful construction of the entrances, the ceiling, the walls, and the floor are important elements for the creation of a comfortable microclimatic environment in the teachers' lounge.

**The Functional Aspect:** The nature of the activities taking place in the teachers' lounge have to be taken into consideration. At times, due to the fact that some of these activities may occur simultaneously, separate areas have to be established within the room. These subdivisions need to be constructed and located carefully so they will be appropriate to the relevant activity, and not infringe on other people's space. The separation between different corners can be facilitated by the use of different lights and movable furniture, in order to create an atmosphere of physical separation and privacy while not shutting out or intruding on people outside the setting. The "meeting-corner," for instance, might be in a "living room" mode, with low sofas placed around a low table, creating a desirable sense of both comfort and privacy. The "teacher-parent meeting corner" might serve as one of the places for resting; however, it is important to locate it close to the entrance yet detached from it, in order to ensure privacy when conversing. Teachers could carry out their individual work while sitting at higher tables located all around the room, or in one corner of the room referred to as the "individual work corner," which might consist of a counter constructed along the wall. It is important to supply each unit with suitable lighting, for this serves to create a sense of distinctive functions. Partial separation of different areas can be accomplished by constructing low partitions, or movable cupboards.

The distinction between the design of a "living room" corner and a "work corner" in the lounge can have important implications for the kind of "niche" inhabited by the teachers, and will determine their accommodation to the realities of their environment. In the absence of some kind of a "living room" component, for example, it will be difficult for teachers to enjoy the rest function of the lounge. The ensuing ecological conditions might be conceived as encouraging teachers to focus more on the "work" function of the lounge. Thus, one may conclude that the environment of the lounge, as an ecological niche, is shaped both by a perception of its function, and by the accommodation of its inhabitants to this reality.

# Appendix II

## Questionnaire

Dear Teacher,

We would be grateful if you would take some time to respond to the enclosed questionnaire. We are conducting a research project on the functions of teachers' lounges, and your assistance would be greatly appreciated.

Sincerely yours,

Professor Miriam Ben-Peretz
Dr. Shifra Schonmann

School of Education
University of Haifa

## Part A: Characteristics of Teachers' Lounges

The following is a list of the characteristics of teachers' lounges.

Please note for each, on a scale from 1 to 5, how closely each characteristic describes the teachers' lounge in your school.

1 – is **not true** or **very seldom true** for the teachers' lounge in my school
2 – is **seldom true** for the teachers' lounge in my school
3 – ism **sometimes true** for the teachers' lounge in my school
4 – is **often true** for the teachers' lounge in my school
5 – is **very often true** for the teachers' lounge in my school

## Characteristics

1. Pleasant atmosphere
2. Expansive, lots of space
3. A great deal of information communicated
4. Noisy
5. Humor
6. Overflowing with students
7. Competitive environment
8. Regular seating arrangement
9. Colorful
10. Leadership is established
11. Sharing of secrets
12. The principal drops in
13. Tolerance
14. Professional competitiveness
15. Lessons are prepared
16. Tests are graded
17. A place to talk with parents
18. A place to talk with students
19. A place to talk with colleagues
20. A place to rest

## Part B: Domains of Impact of Teacher' Lounges

What is the extent of the impact of the teachers' lounge on different domains of school life? Please note your estimate in the table.

| | Domains | no impact | very little impact | some impact | considerable impact | great impact |
|---|---|---|---|---|---|---|
| 1. | Developing educational activities | | | | | |
| 2. | Individual treatment of students | | | | | |
| 3. | Developing interpersonal relationships among teachers | | | | | |
| 4. | Management of professional problems | | | | | |
| 5. | Management of administrative problems | | | | | |
| 6. | Improving school climate | | | | | |
| 7. | Promoting motivation for work | | | | | |
| 8. | Improving relationships between teachers and principal | | | | | |
| 9. | Improving communication | | | | | |
| 10. | Collaboration between colleagues | | | | | |

Please give a concrete example for any domain you choose.

## Part C: Demographic Details

•

## Part D: Open-ended Opportunities to Write about the Lounge, and to Provide a Metaphor Describing It

# References


Acker, S. (1988): Teachers Gender and Resistance. *British Journal of Sociology of Education* 9, 3:307–322.

Ball, S. M. (1987): *The Micro-Politics of the School.* London: Methuen.

Bell, B. & Gilbert, J. (1994): Teacher Development as Professional, Personal, and Social Development. *Teaching and Teacher Education* 10, 5:483–497.

Ben-Peretz, M. (1995): *Learning from Experience: Memory and the Teacher's Account of Teaching.* Albany, NY: SUNY Press.

———. (1996): *Women as Teachers: Teachers as Women.* London: Falmer Press, pp. 178–186.

Berliner, C. D. (1990): If the Metaphor Fits, Why Not Wear It? The Teacher as Executive. *Theory into Practice,* 2: 85–93.

Black, M. (1979): More about Metaphors. In: A. Orthony (Ed.) *Metaphor and Thought.* Cambridge: Cambridge University Press.

Blass, N. & Avram, S. (1988): *Staffroom* [in Hebrew].

Boyce, S. N. (1987): *Welcome to the Theatre.* Chicago, Nelson Hall.

Brinker, M. (1984): *Aesthetics as a Method of Inquiry.* Tel Aviv: Ministry of Defense [in Hebrew].

Britzman, D. P. (1986): Cultural Myths in the Making of a Teacher: Biography and Social Structure in Teacher Education. *Harvard Educational Review* 56, 4:442–455.

Bruner, J. (1996): *The Culture of Education.* Cambridge, MA: Harvard University Press.

Burgess, R. & Gaudy, P. (1986): *Time for Drama.* Milton Keynes, Philadelphia: Open University Press.

Casey, K. & Apple M. W. (1984): Gender and the Conditions of Teachers' Work: The Development of Understanding in America. In: S. Acker (Ed.) *Teacher, Gender and Careers.* London: Falmer Press.

Clandinin, D. J. (1986): *Classroom Practice: Teacher Images in Action.* London and Philadelphia: The Falmer Press.

Clandinin, D. J. & Connelly, F. M. (1986): Teachers' Personal Practical Knowledge: Image and Narrative Unity. Working paper.

———. (1986): Rhythm in Teaching: The Narrative Study of Teachers' Personal Knowledge of Classrooms. *Teaching and Teacher Education,* 2, 4:377–87.

———. (1995): *Teachers' Professional Knowledge Landscapes.* New York and London: Teachers College Press.

Collins, E. C. & Green, J. L. (1990): Metaphors: The Construction of a Perspective. *Theory into Practice,* 2: 71–77.

Connelly, F. M. & Clandinin, D. J. (1990): The Cyclic Temporal Structure of Schooling. In: M. Ben-Peretz & R. Bromme (Eds.) *The Nature of Time in Schools.* New York and London: Teachers College Press, pp. 36–63.

———. (1985): Personal Practical Knowledge and the Modes of Knowing: Relevance for Teaching and Learning. *NSSE Yearbook,* 84 2:174–98.

———. (1986): On Narrative Method, Personal Philosophy, and Narrative Units in the Story of Teaching. *Journal of Research in Science Teaching,* 23, 3:15–32.

Corrie, L. (1996): Subversives in the Staffroom: Resolution of Knowledge Conflicts among Teaching Colleagues. *Teaching and Teacher Education,* 12, 3: 235 247.

Cunningham, W. C. & Gresso, D. W. (1993): *Cultural Leadership: The Culture of Excellence in Education.* Boston, MA: Allyn and Bacon.

Dreeben, R. (1970): *The Nature of Teaching,* Glenview, IL: Scott, Foolsman.

Eisner, E. W. (1998): *The Kind of Schools We Need.* Portsmouth, NH: Heineman.

Feiman-Nemser, S. & Floden, R. E. (1986): The Cultures of Teaching. In: M. C. Wittrock (Ed.) *Handbook of Research on Teaching.* New York: MacMillan, pp. 505–525.

Fish, S. (1980): *Is There a Text in This Class.* Boston: Harvard University Press.

Fullan, M. G. (1995): The Limits and the Potential of Professional Development. In: T. R. Guskey & M. Huberman (Eds.) *Professional Development in Education.* New York: Teachers College Press, pp. 253–67.

Fullan, M. & Hargreaves, A. (1996): *What's Worth Fighting For? Working Together for Your School.* New York: Teachers College Press.

Goffman, E. (1959): *The Presentation of Self in Everyday Life.* New York: Doubleday, Anchor.

Goodlad, J. I. & Klein, F. (1970): *Behind the Classroom Door.* Worthington, OH: James.

Gordon, D. (1996): The Nature of the Relationship Between Pre- and In-Service Teacher Education. Paper presented at the MOFET Institution, Tel-Aviv, the 7th of May 1996.

Grimmet, P. P. & Crehan, E. P. (1992): The Nature of Collegiality in Teacher Development: The Case of Clinical Supervision. In: A. Hargreaves & M. G. Fullan (Eds.) *Understanding Teacher Development.* New York: Teachers College Press, pp. 56–85.

Gross, E. (1949): *Informal Relations and the Social Organization of Work in an Industrial Office.* Unpublished Ph.D. dissertation, Department of Sociology, University of Chicago.

Hall, E. T. (1959): *The Silent Language.* New York: Garden City.

Hall, G. E. & Rutherford, W. L. (1983): *Three Change Facilitator Styles: How Principals Affect Improvement Efforts.* Austin, TX: University of Texas, Research and Development Center for Teacher Education.

Hammersley, M. (1984): Staffroom News. In: *Classrooms and Staffrooms,* Milton Keynes, UK: Open University Press, pp. 203–214.

Hargreaves, A. (1989): Contrived Collegiality and the Culture of Teaching. Paper presented at the annual meeting of the Canadian Society for the Study of Education, Quebec City.

———. (1992): Cultures of Teaching: A Focus for Change. In: A. Hargreaves & M. G. Fullan (Eds.) *Understanding Teacher Development.* New York: Teachers College Press, pp. 216–240.

Hargreaves, A. & Woods, P. (Eds.) (1984): *Classrooms and Staffrooms.* Milton Keynes, UK: Open University Press.

Hargreaves, D. H., Hester, S. K., & Mellor, F. J. (1984): Rules in Play. In: A. Hargreaves & P. Woods (Eds.) *Classrooms and Staffrooms.* Milton Keynes, UK: Open University Press, pp. 25–35.

Hornbrook, D. (1989): *Education and Dramatic Art.* Oxford: Basil Blackwell.

Jackson, P. W. (1968): *Life in Classrooms.* New York: Holt, Reinhart & Winston.

———. (1986): *The Practice of Teaching.* New York: Teachers College Press, Columbia University.

Katriel, T. (1991): *Communal Webs.* Albany, NY: SUNY Press.

Katriel, T. & Nesher, P. (1986): Gibush: The Rhetoric Cohesion in Israeli School Culture. *Comparative Education Review,* 30, 2: 216–232.

Keinan, A. (1994): *The Staffroom: Observing the Professional Culture of Teachers.* Brock Field, U.K.: Ashgall Publishing.

Lakoff, G. & Johnson, M. (1980): *Metaphors We Live By.* Chicago: University of Chicago Press.

Lampert, M. & Loewenberg-Ball, D. (1998): *Teaching Multimedia and Mathematics.* New York: Columbia University, Teachers College Press.

Lieberman, A. & Miller, L. (1984): *Teachers, Their World, and Their Work.* Alexandria, VA: ASCD.

Little, J. W. (1982): Norms of Collegiality and Experimentation: Workplace Conditions of School Success. *American Education Research Journal,* 19, 3: 325–340.

———. (1987): Teachers as Colleagues. In: V. R. Kohl (Ed.) *Educators' Handbook: A Research Perspective.* New York: Longman, pp. 491–548.

———. (1990): The Persistence of Privacy: Autonomy and Initiative in Teachers' Professional Relations. *Teachers College Record,* 91, 4: 509–536.

Lortie, D. (1975): *Schoolteacher.* Chicago: University of Chicago Press.

Louis, M. R. (1996): Acculturation in the Workplace: Newcomers as Lay Ethnographers. In: B. Schneider (Ed.) *Organizational Climate and Culture.* San Francisco: Jossey-Bass, pp. 85–129.

Lyman, S. M. & Scott, M. B. (1975): *The Drama of Social Reality.* New York: Oxford University Press.

McLaughlin, M. W. (1994): Strategic Sites for Teacher's Professional Development. In: P. P. Grimmett & J. Neufeld (Eds.) *Teacher Development and the Struggle for Authority.* New York: Teachers College Press, pp. 31–51.

Mead, G. A. (1934): *Mind, Self and Society.* Chicago: University of Chicago Press.

Middleton, D. & Edwards, D. (Eds.) (1990): *Collective Remembering.* London: Sage.

Munby, H. & Russell, T. (1990): Metaphor in the Study of Teachers' Professional Knowledge. *Theory into Practice,* 2: 116–121.

O'Toole, J. (1992): *The Process of Drama.* London: Routledge.

Orr, J. E. (1990): Sharing Knowledge Celebrating Identity: Community Memory in a Service Culture. In: D. Middleton & D. Edwards (Eds.) *Collective Remembering.* London: Sage, pp. 169–189.

Rap, U. (1973): *Sociology and Theatre.* Tel Aviv: Tel Aviv University [in Hebrew].

Richardson, D. M., Short, M. P., & Prickett, L. R. (1993): *School Principals and Change.* New York: Garland Publication, Inc.

Robbins, P. & Alvy, H. B. (1995): *The Principal's Companion-Strategies and Hints to Make the Job Easier.* London: Corwin Press.

Rosenholtz, S. J. (1989): *Teachers' Workplace: The Social Organization of Schools.* New York and London: Teachers College Press.

Rubin, R., Avram, S., & Avner, A. (1984): *Staffroom.* Tel-Aviv [in Hebrew].

Sarason, S. B. (1972): *The Culture of the School and the Problem of Change.* Boston: Allyn and Bacon.

———. (1996): *Revisiting the Culture of the School and the Problem of Change.* New York: Teachers College Press.

Schonmann, S. (1995): Between Text and Counter Text: Theatre in Search of Political Meaning. *Contemporary Theatre Review,* 3, 2:175–183.

Schonmann, S. & Ben-Peretz, M. (1993): Principal's Involvement in the Teacher's Lounge and Its Implications. *Studies in Educational Administration and Organization,* 19: 5–28 [in Hebrew].

Schunk, D. H. (1991): *Learning Theories: An Educational Perspective.* New York: Merrill.

Schwab, J. J. (1964): Problems, Topics, and Issues. In: S. Elam (Ed.) *Education and the Structure of Knowledge.* Chicago, Rand McNally, pp. 4–47.

———. (1970): *The Practical: A Language for Curriculum.* Washington, D.C.: National Education Association.

———. (1978): Eros and Education. In: J. Westbury & N. J. Wilkof (Eds.) *Science, Curriculum and Liberal Education Selected Essays.* Chicago: University of Chicago Press.

Shapiro, Y. & Ben-Eliezer, U. (1991): *Elements of Sociology.* Tel-Aviv: Am Oved [in Hebrew].

Shipman, M. D. (1986): *Sociology of the School.* Jerusalem: Academon [in Hebrew].

Smylie, M. A. (1995): Teacher Learning in the Workplace. In T. R. Guskey & M. Huberman (Eds.) *Professional Development in Education.* New York: Teachers College Press, pp. 92–113.

Spolin, V. (1973): *Improvisation for the Theatre.* Evanston, IL: Northwestern University Press.

Talbert, J. E. & McLaughlin, M. W. (1994): Teacher Professionalism in Local School Contexts. *American Journal of Education,* 102:123–153.

Toulmin, S. (1980): The Charm of the Scout. New York Review of Books, April 3.

Turner, V. (1976): *Dramas, Fields and Metaphors.* Ithaca, NY: Cornell University Press.

Vaughn, J. A. (1978): *Drama A to Z.* New York: Frederick Unger Publishing.

Weber, M. (1968): *Economy and Society.* New York: Bedminster Press.

Wolfe, M. & Proshansky, H. (1974): The Physical Setting as a Factor in Group Function and Process. In: J. Lang, C. Burnette, W. Moleski, & P. Vachon (Eds.) *Designing for Human Behavior.* Stroudberg, PA: Dowden, Hutchinson & Ross, p. 220–235.

Woods, P. (1984): The Meaning of Staffroom Humour. In: A. Hargreaves & P. Woods (Eds.) *Classrooms & Staffrooms.* Milton Keynes, UK: Open University Press, pp. 190–203.

Zerubavel, E. (1981): *Hidden Rhythms.* Berkeley, CA: University of California Press.

———. (1979): *Patterns of Time in Hospital Life: A Sociological Perspective.* Chicago and London: University of Chicago Press.

# Index